IMAGINARY WORLDS
notes on a new curriculum

Richard Murphy

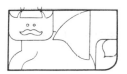

Teachers&Writers

Fifth printing

ACKNOWLEDGMENTS

We are grateful to the publishers of the following books for permission to reprint passages which appear in this publication:

A BARBARIAN IN ASIA by Henri Michaux, excerpt from preface to the American edition, translated by Sylvia Beach. Copyright 1949 by New Directions Publishing Corp., reprinted by permission of New Directions.

SLAUGHTER-HOUSE FIVE, OR THE CHILDREN'S CRUSADE by Kurt Vonnegut, Jr. Copyright (c) 1969 by Kurt Vonnegut, Jr. A Seymour Lawrence Book/Delacorte Press.

THE LION, THE WITCH AND THE WARDROBE, Book I in the CHRONICLES OF NARNIA by C.S. Lewis. Reprinted with permission of the Macmillan Company, copyright 1950 by the Macmillan Company.

"Those Places They Call Schools", by Robert Coles. Reprinted by permission of the Harvard Educational Review, copyright 1970 by the President and Fellows of Harvard College, Cambridge, Massachusetts.

Thanks also to David Shapiro for permission to reprint "Learn Something, America", written by David Shapiro and the Writers' Workshop at MUSE (Brooklyn Childrens' Museum); and to Miss Shelly Kintisch, a teacher at I.S. 70, Manhattan, for letting Richard Murphy work with two of her classes.

The original publication of this book was made possible by a grant from the New York State Council on the Arts. It is now reprinted through a grant from the National Endowment for the Arts.

Cover design by Adalberto Ortiz

INTRODUCTION

Last winter I began a series of weekly visits to one sixth grade and one eighth grade class at I.S. 70 in Manhattan. I had had little previous experience in classroom teaching and none at all with these particular grades. I chose to work along with a social studies teacher, Miss Shelly Kintisch, rather than with a member of the English department, and we agreed that I would conduct one class a week, consisting of a forty-five minute period, for each of the two grades. My initial work with Utopias was adapted to this rather traditional classroom setting, but aside from the discomfort I felt in being cast in a traditional teacher's role—the absurdity of having to address twenty to thirty children all at once—I did not immediately foresee the problems that would result from this approach. It was only later, after the children had started writing, that I realized the project would require far more intimate and flexible contact with children, and a setting which provided ample opportunity for individual conferences, encouragement and criticism.

I can say with some confidence that the ideal setting for a Utopias project would be an open classroom where children are given wide latitude in selecting from a variety of activities which are in progress simultaneously. In such a classroom a teacher could approach a child with the suggestion that he explore, and perhaps write about, one of his interests of the moment. If his activity attracts other children and a cluster of devotees seems to emerge, it might then be appropriate to develop an "Imaginary Worlds Corner" where children could read samples of Utopian literature (including the work of other children), where they could write themselves, or begin any number of projects in the visual arts—such as constructing a model city—related to the theme. In short, this procedure would allow children to pursue their own private directions with the help of a teacher, but without undue pressure.

I have not had the opportunity to work in such a setting. In the one case where I was able to work with a small group of children (the sixth graders) by myself, I knew that they had come with me because they were willing to write. Had I been able to offer a variety of physical materials for drawing and constructing, I might have been able to attract other children. But in an intermediate school or high school, where children must change classes, there is simply no space that they can call their own. Materials are inevitably lost or stolen, and I often wondered if teachers couldn't be made to move from room to room instead. As a result, I have little to suggest to the teacher who is aware of the visual and physical realities of the theme except to say that there is a wealth of material and ideas for someone to develop, in an appropriate setting. I was particularly interested in, and would refer any interested teacher to Paul Goodman's writing on city planning (*Communitas* and *Utop-*

ian Essays and Practical Proposals and numerous magazine articles) and the work of many modern architects such as Paolo Soleri who are involved in planning cities of the future.

I was aware from the beginning just how massive the general notion of Utopias might seem to children, and how overwhelming. I wanted to avoid the possibility of confusing or intimidating the children with infinite possibilities, and to limit the abstraction I felt certain could lead only to cliches and banality ("In my Utopia no one would fight. Different races would all get along together. And there would be no pollution.") For this reason I began my work at I. S. 70 by focusing on smaller, more manageable topics. In my preparatory reading of Utopian literature I had searched for discrete ideas, common to all Utopias, which seemed powerful and emotional enough to be discussed in relative isolation. And for each topic I tried to find a suitable literary example. With the sixth graders I even avoided the term "Utopia" during the early stages of the project, preferring to talk only of "imaginary worlds." I developed a list of such ideas, which is by no means comprehensive and could be expanded in any number of directions. Because of the large number of children I had to involve from the beginning (or lose them as children can get lost in classrooms) I began with the idea of traveling to imaginary worlds. The idea had immediate appeal, was basic to the continuing theme and was, of course, a logical starting point.

Here is the list:

Traveling to Utopia
Landscape
Architecture
Population distribtuion
Sports and recreation
Labor
Technology (or absence
    of it)
Child rearing and
    family units
Education
Religion (official or
    practiced)
Crime and punishment
Sexual mores and
    taboos

Economics (distribution
    of land, wealth, etc.)
Governmental structure
    (democracy, monarchy,
    oligarchy, etc.)
War
Foreign policy
Laws and human rights
    (constitutions)
Assumptions regarding
    the nature of man
The artist in Utopia
The reverse view: our
    society as seen from
    Utopia

Originally I thought that a clever ordering of these discrete topics would provide the impetus for larger worlds, and that the children would view each new topic as a small "chapter" which potentially could be joined to others. In time I came to see this as a rather simplistic notion. After three or four sessions I felt that my suggestions for new chapters were actually interfering with directions the children might have taken on their own, thus delaying the independence that I sought. I hope that the diaries that follow show a gradual movement away from the list, for I came to think of it primarily as a useful way of getting started and of introducing children to the theme in a way that is not intimidating. It was not the key to meaningful longer works; that depended, I learned, on approaching each child's work on its own terms.

Richard Murphy
Summer 1971

. . .I have certainly made propaganda, after my own fashion, for an endless variety of civilizations. (Down with the idea of only one!) There have been decades and decades of them. There could be, there can be more and more of them. Just as each child must make up his own personality out of a thousand different elements and a few chromosomes of various types, so the masses of men must make up a personality that will be called their civilization. A miners' union calls a strike—good. But suppose that instead they were to declare a miners' civilization. How strange it would be. What a lot we should have to learn from them. Wouldn't they shake us. And then we could have a South Pole civilization. Why not a Tennessee Valley civilization too?

The most urgently needed science is one that will *show us how to make civilizations.*

—Henri Michaux

VCgift

Table of Contents

Introduction   3

Traveling to an Imaginary Place   9

Imaginary States 22

Religion 29

Question of Continuity in Writing 35

War 37

Moving Toward A Variety of Topics 46

Ann 48

Lisa 55

Jeff 58

Schools 64

The SUTEC Workshop 77

Henry Sneed 90

Discovering Our World Neighbors 101

Bibliography 108

THE NIGHTMARE WORLD

I am a very queery, dreary eater
Eating snake eyes, and ant skin froggy
Legs, pickles and eggs slimy
Wormy chocolate gooey covered
Pickle cream Echy Ecchy Ecchy
Burp Glurp Chirp Bubble "Whew"!

Fred Wolf
Eighth Grade

Traveling to an Imaginary Place

Like the old story about getting married—I have the horrible premonition that I will simply run out of things to say. I've asked for a record player which is nowhere visible in the room and this increases my anxiety. Miss Kintisch sits at her desk. She has told the kids only that I would be coming in to do something special. (I preferred an open-ended introduction to something which might define the work too narrowly, but now I wonder if I can live up to this introduction.) The class quiets down on its own, then the record player appears. I ask the kids to form a circle around it. Suddenly there is a tremendous banging of chairs and tables. . . I'm sinking. But once again the kids quiet down without a word from me or Miss Kintisch.

I introduce myself, careful to point out that I am not a teacher (more for my sake that theirs?), that I am interested in children's writing, etc. I say that I'll be coming in once a week, and that what we'll be doing isn't very close to geography (some sighs of relief at this), but is close to something I had observed the class doing last week. They had been working on map reading, and the homework assignment was to make up their own continent, complete with legend describing population, climate, etc.—a nice assignment, and one that I might like to go back to with specific reference to their own Utopian writing. From there I introduce the idea of writing about an imaginary world. I say that today we just want to talk and write about ways to get there. Later we will discuss the people we meet, how they live, etc.

I point out that a lot of people have written about imaginary worlds, and that until about a hundred years ago the way they usually got there was by boat. There would be a storm, they would get lost, and suddenly find themselves in a place no one had ever discovered before. I say that today we have many different ways of traveling to such a place, and ask the kids for ideas. They respond immediately with enthusiasm: submarine, spaceship, airplane, you could get hijacked. Then I ask if there are ways of traveling without gadgets—"swim". But what about traveling in your own head—"dreams, imagination". You could also travel into the future, one kid says. Great! Does he know a book called *The Time Machine*? He does. I say that I had planned to read a few pages from it today. We turn out the lights and turn on the record player—Eliot Carter's *Double Concerto* which I describe as imaginary world music—too bad for Carter. I read from the opening pages of Wells' book:

It was at ten o'clock today that the first of all Time Machines began its career. I gave it a last tap, tried all the screws again, put one more drop of oil on the quartz rod, and sat myself in the saddle. I suppose a suicide who holds a pistol to his skull feels much the same wonder at what will come next as I felt then. I took the starting lever in one hand and the stopping one in the other, pressed the first, and almost immediately the second. I seemed to reel; I felt a nightmare sensation of falling; and, looking round, I saw the laboratory exactly as before. Had anything happened? For a moment I suspected that my intellect had tricked me. Then I noted the clock. A moment before, as it seemed, it had stood at a minute or so past ten; now it was nearly half-past three!

I drew my breath, set my teeth, gripped the starting lever with both hands, and went off with a thud. The laboratory got hazy and went dark. Mrs. Watchett came in and walked, apparently without seeing me, towards the garden door. I suppose it took her a minute or so to traverse the place, but to me she seemed to shoot across the room like a rocket. I pressed the lever over to its extreme position. The night came like the turning out of a lamp, and in another moment came to-morrow. The laboratory grew faint and hazy, then fainter and ever fainter. To-morrow night came black, then day again, night again, day again, faster and faster still. An eddying murmur filled my ears, and a strange, dumb confusedness descended on my mind.

I am afraid I cannot convey the peculiar sensations of time travelling. They are excessively unpleasant. There is a feeling exactly like that one has upon a switchback—of a helpless headlong motion! I felt the same horrible anticipation, too, of an imminent smash. As I put on pace, night followed day like the flapping of a black wing. The dim suggestion of the laboratory seemed presently to fall away from me, and I saw the sun hopping swiftly across the sky, leaping it every minute, and every minute marking a day. I supposed the laboratory had been destroyed and I had come into the open air. I had a dim impression of scaffolding, but I was already going too fast to be conscious of any moving things. The slowest snail that ever crawled dashed by too fast for me. The twinkling succesion of darkness and light was excessively painful to the eye. Then, in the intermittent darkness, I saw the moon spinning swiftly through her quarters from new to full, and had a faint glimpse of the circling stars. Presently, as I went on, still gaining velocity, the palpitation of night and day merged into one continuous greyness; the sky took on a wonderful deepness of blue, a splendid luminous color like that of early twilight; the jerking sun became a streak of fire, a brilliant arch, in space; the moon a fainter fluctuating band; and I could see nothing of the stars, save now and then a brighter circle flickering in the blue.*

Then I ask the kids to return to their desks to write about their own way of traveling to an imaginary place.

The music continues. But some of the kids want the lights back on. There is once again a lot of crashing and banging of chairs but, to my surprise, nearly all the kids get out paper and begin writing. I spend the rest of the class circulating, as much as possible, from desk to desk. The sixth graders are very demanding, and there are always four or five hands raised. Sometimes I am asked to clarify the assignment, sometimes for a spelling word (they don't believe me when I tell them in all honesty that my spelling is horrible), sometimes I am asked just to read what they have written. One piece begins "I have a knapsack on my back, and my wings are being put into place. I don't know where I'm going." I'm feeling great.

Toward the end of the class I discover real personal deficiencies in what educators call, I think, classroom management. Some of the kids want to keep working on the assignment, rather than hand it in to me. Their enthusiasm amazes me but I worry that pieces will be lost. I try to collect as many papers as I can in the chaos that follows, but allow a few of the kids to escape with their Utopias stuffed haphazardly in their notebooks. I wonder if I will ever see these.

After my session with the sixth graders, Miss Kintisch suggested that some movement away from a fairy tale, enchanted wonderland type of presentation might be more appropriate for her eighth grade class. This strikes me as exactly what is needed, but I'm not certain I can achieve it. I don't want to make the idea of imaginary worlds too intellectual, at least in these early sessions. Also, I want to retain all the elements of the previous presentation, the discussion of ways to get to an imaginary place, the reading of *The Time Machine*. Finally, I decide there is a good chance that some of the eighth graders already know *The Time Machine*, since at least one sixth grader did, and that some discussion of *why* the book was written might be appropriate.

I begin by introducing myself as before (not a teacher) and asking the group to form a circle. They do so much more efficiently than the sixth graders, so quickly in fact that I am left looking in from the outside, and there is no way in! None of the open classroom experts ever warned me that this would happen. Finally, I squeeze through a couple of desks, to the great amusement of the kids, and we are off on a discussion of traveling to imaginary places. It is basically the same discussion (the only exception being

---

*From H.G. Wells' *The Time Machine*. Bantam Books, 1968. Pp. 20-22

that these kids are fully aware of the possibilities of using drugs for such purposes) but the atmosphere is quite different. The eighth graders are wiser, they've learned not to trust outsiders, not to give completely of themselves as the sixth graders seem to—and the discussion is a little reserved as they rattle off the many ways of traveling to imaginary places.

They are on to the idea of time travel quickly, and I use this to introduce the fact that I'm going to read from *The Time Machine.* But first I ask how many have actually read the book or seen the movie. I still don't know the answer for this, since it appears there are numerous variations upon the original theme. And some of the kids are already reeling off, for instance, the plot to the recent Star Trek show. We run through a few such plots, then I begin the discussion of Wells.

I mention that when the time traveler begins his trip, he is very excited about being the first man to look into a future in which men will have vastly improved their condition. He expects the future to be perfectly marvelous. Instead, he finds a very frightening world—the decayed English upper class and the underground workers. Then I use a metaphor which I had thought of the night before, but which worries me because I think it may be too difficult. I say that writing about an imaginary world is like holding a trick mirror before society. Everything is distorted but it is still you in front of that mirror. A newspaper reporter, writing at the same time as Wells, might have said "conditions among the working class in England are terrible, while the upper classes get richer and lazier." That would be like a regular mirror. But the imaginary world mirror distorts as it shows us the upper class—pale, deadly white, child-like, defenseless. I can't be sure, but I have the feeling that the kids are still with me. In any case, we've come a long way from fairy tales.

I read from *The Time Machine* as before, then ask the kids to begin writing. Most of them do, though there are a few whom I have failed to reach at all. The atmosphere in this class is so different that I suddenly feel a sense of enormous failure. And there is nothing to do. The eighth graders don't ask questions or raise their hands. So I circulate on my own, which is much harder, trying to encourage those who are not writing. When the class is over, I am surprised by the number of pieces that are turned in.

TWO OF THE SIXTH GRADE PIECES:

As the last bit of orange turned blue in the sky I set out.

I walked till I met the water, I leaped to where I left my boat and as the first morning breeze came the boat sailed away carrying me far far away.

We sailed days & days until we reached the rainbow sky. The color lifted us up up up . . .

Till we came upon a city made of GOLD AND SILVER.

The city twinkled as the sunset fell. My boat nested in the harbor as I went on the shore.

I walked down the streets and everything was made from gold. I went over to the inn and the Keeper let me in. He gave me a golden key to my golden room.

As I reach my room and there I find that everything was silver, even my bed!

I sleeped that night and in the morning my body was all bronze.

I took a swim that afternoon but when I came out of the pool my body was all gold so I went home across the sea.

And I got home just in time to hear my mother tell me to get up & get dressed for breakfast.

Ann Turner

THE DOLL

It was a Sunday evening at about 8:32 when my Uncle came to visit me, he was an older man about 73 (I am 30) with white hair, he was bent over, kind of a hunch back without the bump on his back. He was short and very thin. He has given me a doll, right now I am looking at the doll. It's not an ordinary type of thing, it's rather mysterious. It's very old, wearing a long dress. Part of the doll's hair was tied up, most of it was hanging down the sides of its face. I've thought of a name for it, Rachel.

My Uncle has gone home now so I am taking my doll into my room with me.

Now it is much later in the evening and I have propped my doll up in the corner of my room on my bed table (which is next to my bed). I take a last look at Rachel and go to sleep with a vision of her in my head.

Strange things began happening when I was falling asleep, at first flashes of bright red, blue, white, yellow, purple, crimson, scarlet and green. Then I began to see the whole day over again in slow motion, but every time I saw myself I was holding the doll! Then things got blurred and got bigger, then they would stare at me, even the me in the dream would stare at me, but the doll, I didn't have the doll earlier in the day,

In the dream Rachel seemed life-like, it would look at me when I asked myself something, as if it were telling me something. About ten minutes before my Uncle came (in the dream) I woke up.

Strange enough, I wasn't in my room anymore. Even stranger enough I was in my bed and right next to me was my night table. With the doll on it. It was sitting there, staring at me, and it wasn't in the same position I put it in, but so I wouldn't scare myself I told myself it was from tossing and turning during the dream.

I looked around to see where I was. I had been looking around for quite some time now and had been, and started crying. (I can't help it if that's the type of person I am.) I had finally figured out where I am.

There are lots of round basketball type things (only bigger) and the background is such a deep blue it's almost black.

Right now I'm floating helplessly in outer space with that doll I named Rachel, my bed, and my doom.

The End

Victoria Larkin

SEVERAL OF THE EIGHTH GRADE "UTOPIAS":

YEAR: 100,196

It all started one day when I was swimming in the ocean at Miami Beach. And then I got deeper and deeper, I could feel the pressure. Suddenly I felt myself out of air. Then I saw a wide-eyed man in an air-tight cave. I swam over there for he had power over me. We got in and all of a sudden I could breathe again.

He said, "Would you like to see the future?"

I was curious and I said, "Yes." And in this air-tight cave underwater he pulled out a stone and we walked through. The first thing I saw was my grave:

FRED ZYDEL
BORN 1957
DIED 2037

Then I glanced over to my left and I saw another grave but this one read—

CECILIA GLADORE
BORN 2007
DIED 2109

This really got me because I saw that we were possibly more than 250 years in the future. Then I walked out of the graveyard. The sign—which was a source of ultra violet gamma rays that were made from a completely different source of energy that was ever discovered—read,

5000 YEAR OLD GRAVEYARD
FELL: 2200

Then I asked someone, "What's the date?"
He replied, "7221."
The man was 2 feet tall. He had no pinky. No little toe. A big chin, and a gigantic brain. The man looked at me and was startled.
He said,　　　　　　"You belong in a museum.
You went extinct except
about 600,000 of you in
1985 when your primitive
energy usage polluted the
world."
He also said the ones who lived through it decided to start from scratch.
"You were all called:
EARLY HUMAN PHYSICAL
POWER
Which means you still
needed your muscles
to do work."
Then I noticed that all along he wasn't moving his lips when he was talking. And when he was walking his feet weren't moving. He brought me to his city. Then I wondered where did that man go? Well, I didn't worry about it. When I was in the city there was no matter, no solids, liquids, or gasses. Just colors, and they look like buildings, and you can walk in and out of it like looking at an ultra-violet picture. The people there did not litter but were very kind. Then I felt myself walking and walking. But I did not want to walk this way—I was pulled! Then I read a sign on a door:

MUSEUM OF PHYSICAL HISTORY

I was walking in. I did not want.to. A line of about 600 men walked with me and I walked straight on a stand and remained here ever since.

Fred Zydel

15

One day I decided I was going to get away, away from the bad in the world. Maybe if I found a new place and could bring all the good people in the world there, So:

Friday morning Dec. 26, 1970 I took my bike (which I got for Christmas) and went to call for my two friends Judy and Danny. I had told them about it the night before. So we all set off on our bikes to the end of the Hudson River. We knew it was deserted there and we figured maybe we could find the gate to another world.

We decided we would go down to the bottom of the river but if we didn't find the gate we would drown, you see, if you found the gate you could breathe because it had an air lock in it and the new world would have plenty of air. So we rode our bikes into the water and started peddling very fast. Once Judy, that's my girlfriend, got caught in some seaweed and Danny & I had to pull her out. We had gone down very deep after an hour and were beginning to lose our air. Then Danny spotted a huge, silver gate. We knew this had to be it. We opened the gate and all of a sudden our air came back and we could breathe again. This world we saw was beautiful, it was full of trees and grass and so it seemed beautiful people. The people were of all races and colors. But different from our world, were nice to each other. As we came in they immediately offered food and places to rest and enjoy the beauty of the place. As we walked through (we left our bikes at the gate) we saw stores and and schools like our world but everything was warm and beautiful. We then decided that we were going to get the good people from our world and bring them here. We hopped on our bikes and took a breath of air and went back up. We took all our friends and brought them to the river. We went down but had to come up again 'cause we couldn't find the gate.We may never find it again but we will still keep on trying. Who knows what will happen?

Lisa Methfessal

Just because a world is imaginary doesn't mean it's friendly or beautiful. The following story should explain this.

One day a girl was walking through the forests of the Catskills. She was by herself, and it was late, but her love of nature kept her too preoccupied to be scared. Suddenly, she came to a clearing, and in the middle of it was a silver box, as tall as the girl, and there was a red button in the middle. Being the curious person she was, the girl examined, then pushed the button. A bright green ray of light came, and went, the box also disappeared. The girl found herself in a strange, unfamiliar world. It wasn't hideous, or horrible. It just was like nothing she ever saw. There were tall concrete buildings, different heights, but all very tall. Suddenly a man came from one of the structures. He was just a normal man, except for his odd clothes and his orange eyes. He said nothing, but gestured to her to follow him. She followed. He led her into one of the structures and showed her a platform with glass casing. The man snapped his fingers, and now the girl is a favorite attraction of the museum of the strange world.

Colin Klebanoff

It was the night after the 2 murders. And I was walking on the street that the two people were murdered on. (The police couldn't tell if they were female or male because they were beaten to a bloody pulp!) All of a sudden I heard footsteps. I turned around, but I didn't see anybody. Then I started running. Then all of a sudden I fell deeper and deeper. I fell into the earth. Then suddenly I stopped falling and just floated into this unknown place where people were half Black and White (right down the middle). All of a sudden this man started to fight with himself (like black hitting the white). All of a sudden he died from a fractured skull, I guess. And everywhere I went the people were fighting with themselves. It was horrible. I asked somebody to tell me why people did that and he replied, "Because they all have a sickness no human person knows about. That's why the two people here died!" "Leave before you catch it too!" I started to run. I didn't know where I was going. I went CRAZY. I couldn't find my way out then suddenly AHHHHHHHHHH!!!!!!! I couldn't stand it. I started punching myself. I couldn't stop. This force made me punch myself harder and harder. Then suddenly I heard this wicked laugh. This man was standing on a tower. He had a doll that looked like me. He ripped my arm off, my head, etc. Then all of a sudden I felt myself falling apart. I know this man had something to do with my D . . . E . . . A . . . T . . . H . . . .

Becky Harris

Working independently, Miguel Ortiz also gave an imaginary world assignment to his sixth graders at P.S. 54 in the South Bronx. Mr. Ortiz' diary begins:

"I asked the class to make up stories about imaginary places. Places to which one gets by means of magic. They all knew the *Wizard of Oz* so we talked about that as an example. We also discussed *Alice in Wonderland, Through the Looking Glass, The Time Machine*, etc. I also asked them to describe plants and animals that might be found in an imaginary place and got some interesting drawings as a result."

Below are two examples of the imaginary places discovered in Mr. Ortiz' class. The second, "What I Went Through?" incorporates many of the elements of *Alice in Wonderland,* yet seems to us a very fresh and imaginative re-telling.

17

TERROR IN THE YEAR 5000

Once upon a time a man was about to commence upon a scientific experiment. He was building a time machine that would send him 5,000 years into the future. The time 500 hours before he would enter into the future, it was time, he went in and pulled the lever and went into the future where he found himself in world where everything was automatic. Levitation had been discovered and new weapons were made. People were staring at him and he was in a strange jail with buttons on the wall, he pushed one and immediately he was out and he looked at the time watch and it was exactly 2 minutes before he returned. He opened the door which led to a forest and a creature 60 feet high was behind him. He jumped out of its way and it went down a cliff but the fall of the beast was so fierce that the world shook. He laughed. Then all around him were interplanetary creatures of all kinds. He was terrified. Then all of a sudden, a creature 5,000 feet high ate the animal. The man was feeling terrified, and funny—he was disappearing. He was back in 1970. He destroyed his machine and began building a huge teleporter. Which would someday be very useful to the world in the year 5,000 of the galaxy. He was going to leave it in a house of brick and he always remembered his adventure in terror of the year—5,000.

Francisco E. Alvarez

WHAT I WENT THROUGH?

One day my mother told me to clean up my room. As I was cleaning the dresser, suddenly my hand just fell in. I was amazed. Then I tried my whole body. Then I was on my way down some place. When I woke up I saw this talking insect. He was mad at someone. My eyes couldn't believe what I was seeing.

So he looked like he was mad at me, so I started to walk on this strange path. Then I saw a kingdom, well, it looked like a kingdom. So I started to run as fast as I could, but when I got there, it just disappeared into thin air. Then I started to walk again so I saw this rabbit. It was like he was late for something and he was fussing a lot. Then he started to walk towards some kind of palace. Then I started to run after him without him seeing me. He and I went through this glass then I rushed with him. I was spotted by one of the soldier cards. They had swords, too. I was near one, so I held it up and started to fight. I had won. Then a cheese king came out. Then a banana queen came out, too. The king said, "What a good fight." I said, "No." He said, "If you don't be my guard, I will throw you in the dungeon." I still said no. So he told his guard to put me in the dungeon to think about it. So I found a loose bar and took it out. I started to run and run. I got away from the outside guards. I had a bar in my hand to find the place I fell in so I dig and dig, but no use. I saw the guard then. All of a sudden this fairy godfather. Then I said, "Please let me go back." The fairy said, "All right, if you promise not to come back here."

The End

Paul Latten

Rosellen Brown, in the Hopi Workbench, also introduced the idea of imaginary worlds:

"The oldest three are doing what could loosely be called 'utopian' (again, without the label) fantasies and to our delight, two of them, both boys, don't want to hand their work in at the end. They promise they'll go on at home. The third, the oldest girl, who is agonizingly into herself and into Kahlil Gibran, which she spells improperly, I had hoped to prod in a different, more literally "constructive" direction by asking her to create a different world in detail. But she has rather quickly and superficially written yet another painful autobiographically inclined descent into the dark dark self, this one drug-induced. We have already discussed the attractions and dangers of autobiography and she ventured the opinion that such an attempt would only bring out the worst in her; yet here she is again, creating an unpeopled world, drowning in abstractions (HATE) and ideals."

JILL'S WORLD:

I had decided that I wanted out. The plan had been forming in my mind for months, maybe years. I had the exact time, the exact day, even the exact second. Now all I needed was the courage. And I'd have that, in a small amount of time. Two—no, three hours, just sitting here staring at this bottle—this bottle, my key to sunshine. The minute was approaching. Taking it out, with a quick, short breath—in my mouth. Down, down into my body, reaching out and up into my brain. And my journey started.

I was shouting, shrieking down a gray tunnel, with no end in sight. Infinity passed through my brain. I couldn't make out what I was screaming. A blinding flash of orange, and I saw darkness. It wasn't supposed to be. I was still shrieking—just noises. I was being deprived of sight, or reason. Agony—far into a brick wall. And a door. Stumbling up I opened it and fell onto a path of softness—and my mind floated up and left me.

I dreamed of a world
That could not be
Devoid of hate

Devoid of sorrow
Now, total emptiness
Nothing.
I dreamed a world
I awoke on something orange, kind of reddish-orange, that reminded me of something in my old world. Jumped up—slowly—into a reddish mist—screaming out my happiness, I'm out, I am Out. And falling exhausted on the floor laughing. If only I could clear the fog from my mind.

I lay there on my patch of orange, looking at this solid ochre mass over me. Looked a little like marshmallows. And the fog lifted. I stood up, bumping my head on my sky. Venturing out into my infant universe. After walking, skipping around for an hour I saw it. Just standing there, black, cold, hard—labeled HATE in red letters. It was mocking me. It had perforated my skull, and crawled into my world. I ran away, far, in the opposite direction. All emotions contained in small parcels, labeled, mocking me. Sorrow, jealousy, love and dreary paraded past. Just smiling. I was afraid to let them out.

My world
Everything contained
In a box
I had been running—all day, all night—what is time? I don't know any more. I don't believe I know anything. Isn't this what I wanted? NO—I knew something. I knew I wanted out—again. But I was trapped forever. In the bars and swamps of my brain, created from a pill. Artificial horror. Silence.

Jill

NOTE:
A few weeks later, I found a second "travel" piece in C.S. Lewis' *Chronicle of Narnia,* a series of six books published in paperback and recommended to me by Miguel Ortiz. The idea of finding an imaginary world in a clothes closet seems to me so close to children's own fantasies that I want to quote it here, even though I have never read it to children in a classroom. I think the work might be especially exciting for younger children in the earlier elementary grades.

"Of course it *would* be raining!" said Edmond.
"Do stop grumbling, Ed," said Susan. ". . . it will clear up in an hour or so. And in the meantime we're pretty well off. There's a radio and lots of books."
"Not for me," said Peter, "I'm going to explore the house."
Everyone agreed to this and that was how the adventures began. It was the sort of house that you never seem to come to the end of, and it was full of unexpected places. The first few doors they tried led only into spare bedrooms, as everyone had expected that they would; but soon they found a suit of armour; and after that there was a room

all hung with green, with a harp in one corner; and then they came three steps down and five steps up, and then a kind of little upstairs hall and a door that led out onto a balcony, and then a whole series of rooms that led into each other and were lined with books—most of them very old books and some bigger than a Bible in a church. And shortly after that they looked into a room that was quite empty except for one big wardrobe; the sort that has a looking-glass in the door. There was nothing else in the room at all except a blue-bottle on the windowsill.

"Nothing there!" said Peter, and they all trooped out again—all except Lucy. She stayed behind because she thought it would be worthwhile trying the door of the wardrobe, even though she felt almost sure that it would be locked. To her surprise it opened quite easily, and two moth-balls dropped out.

Looking into the inside, she saw several coats hanging up—mostly long fur coats. There was nothing Lucy liked so much as the smell and feel of fur. She immediately stepped into the wardrobe and got in among the coats and rubbed her face against them, leaving the door open, of course, because she knew that it is very foolish to shut oneself into any wardrobe. Soon she went further in and found that there was a second row of coats hanging up behind the first one. It was almost quite dark in there and she kept her arms stretched out in front of her so as not to bump her face into the back of the wardrobe. She took a step further in—then two or three steps—always expected to feel woodwork against the tips of her fingers. But she could not feel it.

"This must be a simply enormous wardrobe!" thought Lucy, going still further in and pushing the soft folds of the coats aside to make room for her. Then she noticed that there was something crunching under her feet. "I wonder is that more moth-balls?" she thought, stooping down to feel it with her hands. But instead of feeling the hard, smooth wood of the floor of the wardrobe, she felt something soft and powdery and extremely cold. "This is very queer," she said, and went on a step or two further.

Next moment she found that what was rubbing against her face and hands was no longer soft fur but something hard and rough and even prickly. "Why, it is just like branches of trees!" exclaimed Lucy. And then she saw that there was a light ahead of her; not a few inches away where the back of the wardrobe ought to have been, but a long way off. Something cold and soft was falling on her. A moment later she found that she was standing in the middle of a wood at night-time with snow under her feet and snowflakes falling through the air.

Lucy felt a little frightened, but she felt very inquisitive and excited as well. She looked back over her shoulder and there, between the dark tree-trunks, she could still see the open doorway of the wardrobe and even catch a glimpse of the empty room from which she had set out. (She had, of course, left the door open, for she knew that it is a very silly thing to shut oneself into a wardrobe.) It seemed to be still daylight there. "I can always get back if anything goes wrong," thought Lucy. She began to walk forward, crunch-crunch, over the snow and through the wood towards the other light.

Imaginary States

FROM THE DIARIES OF RON PADGETT - P.S. 61 MANHATTAN AND DICK GALLUP - P.S. 20 MANHATTAN

By a happy coincidence, Ron Padgett invented for his class at P.S. 61 an assignment that he called "The State of Poetry." Though not conceived as part of the Utopias project, this assignment fits naturally into the theme, particularly as it was later used by Dick Gallup who interpreted it to mean any imaginary state.

Mr. Padgett describes how he began his assignment:

"I drew a big wobbly screwy shape on the blackboard. What is it? The United States. Good guess. Actually it's just one state. What state? It's not one of the fifty states. It's a state of mind, one kid said. Wow! What a great idea! I said that actually I was thinking of it as the State of Poetry, like a new state added to the Union, the 51st state, but that it exists in our imaginations only. So would they draw a map showing what they thought the State of Poetry. What is it like there? What do things look like? What does the sky look like? etc.

"Jean Morrison held up his hand and said, 'I'd rather write about the State of Shock—it's just like the State of Poetry for most people.' "

SOME EXAMPLES FROM MR. PADGETT'S SIXTH GRADE CLASS:

In the state of poetry people eat poems, it feeds them information how to be a poet. In the capital there is a sign with a rhyme. "Welcome to the capital with your joys and tears and I hope you live happily every single year." The king of the state wears poetry from famous poets. They enjoy their life and that they do indeed, whenever they get lazy they have poetry to read. When they go to bed, all they do is dream. They dream of ice cream and jelly and poetry berries.

Andrew Vecchione

away away my wings
took me
and I flew to the land of poetry
first I crossed to the sun of dreams then I floated to
the moon of sleep   there I rested till morning   then
my feet took me to the Poe mountains   they were
beautiful   then I crossed the sunny land of the pink
people then the dark land of the orange people   I
crossed every thing anyone could wish for in my beautiful land of poetry.

STATE OF POETRY

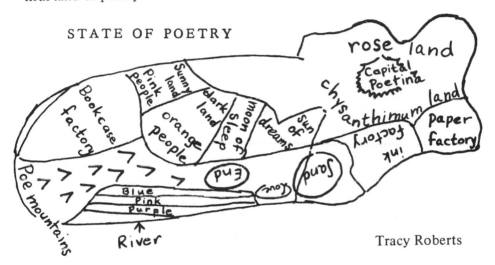

Tracy Roberts

THE STATE OF SHOCK

In the state of shock people are always dreaming.
They can't do anything else.
They dream of future, they dream of past
They dream of the broad area in between
They dream, of cream
They dream of riches. They dream of wisdom
They dream. They are dreaming. For ever.

Jean Morrison

Map Key

capital X
city o
purple grass
blue grass
red grass #
polka dot grass
   is just plain

I live in the state of poetry

It is in outer space
The sky is pink and white and purple polka dots
We have a main power plant shaped like a coil
I live in Wishes
In Wishes wishes come true
My friend lives in Colors
There every body is red and green
My house is a glass ball shaped one
   it isn't green like most of them though.

                          Eliza Bailey

in the
state of
poetry
the people
eat pages
out of books.   they
live in a lot
of different
places to
get inspired.
they never
sleep. They
are all
poets but
no one knows what they
look like.

                          Tommy Kennedy

STATE OF POETRY

The state of Poetry is a place where
the people sit around and write poetry.
They are all very tall with blue eyes, red
hair and glasses.

They are all very smart and they
really live a boring life.

They eat chicken fricksea every day
of their lives.

The only nice part about poetry State
is the yellow orange purple sun and the blue
purple pink sky and the silver grass and the
gold flowers and the black at night and that's
the end.

(unsigned)

PEOPLE IN POETRYLAND

People in poetry land eat peas
People in poetry land play
They play while eating peas
They like Prepared peas while playing with
        pots and pans
Eating peas and playing with pots and pans
        do the Reeble Pals.
Peeble pals eating peas playing with pots
        and pans and writing plays about
        property.
Good-bye Peeple Pal says
see you again in Poetryland.

Myra Morales

An excerpt from Mr. Gallup's diary describing his "lesson" follows, and
finally there are examples of student work from his classes.

"I taught my classes in reverse order today. I began with an idea that
Ron Padgett used at P.S. 61. Ron had drawn an irregular shape on the board
and called it a 'state', eventually making it the 'State of Poetry,' and having

the children write descriptions of the State.

"I began with an irregular shape, which I also called a 'State,' and asked the class to tell me what state it was. They guessed a few states, like Florida, Connecticut, etc.; then Hawaii, Russia, etc.; and finally they started suggesting things like 'Moose horns,' after I had told them it was a 'state of mind.' I suggested the state was 'The State of Poetry,' which they didn't dig too much since they all had ideas of their own. Which is actually an important difference between my teaching methods and those Ron uses. Ron, and Kenneth Koch too, take the kids a good distance into an assignment before they turn them loose. I, on the other hand, begin the assignment and let the kids determine what it is going to be as soon as they can get a take on it at all. Ron's method produces more polished works, while mine produces things that are closer to the children's ideas about form.

"The works produced by this class are really top-notch and I used them to spark a second class. This time I explained the assignment using my own map . . . as usual I got carried away, adding mountains, a lake, a swamp, cities, and a capital, not to mention an airport. Then I used examples from my first class. I should mention the state in the shape of a dollar sign—especially; someone brought up money in connection with the state, so I put a mint into the state, ($ symbol). I threw in a swamp because I like the symbol (🞇) and many children don't know it. I left out roads because it would be too complicated to differentiate them from rivers and coastlines."

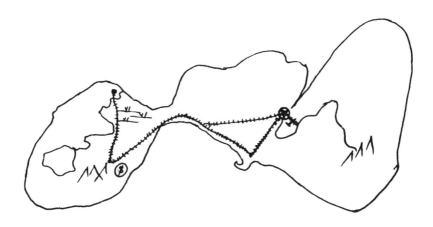

MONELY

To get to Monely you must go to M.T.A. (Monely Transportation Authorities) office at 85 Columbia St., # 20F, in Manhattan. You will be questioned and if we like you we will put you in our "Machine" and you will be in Monely.

Monely is a great state, you don't work, or at least you don't act like it. Everyone picks his own job and believe it or not, things do get done. Many people want to farm but can't but in Monely they get their chance. It is paradise. On weekends you do your own thing. There are no riots, wars, and other primitive acts of violence in Monely. You can't get in unless we're positive you won't cause any sort of trouble. We don't have drugs or anything. If you don't like a simple life, you don't get in. It is exciting however. There's always a good movie. In Moneyland, our new amusement park there are so many things to do, you could go all of your life and never see anything there. There is fishing, boating, hiking, camping, and many other things. If you're ever sick of this world and you want one full of peace, come and see us at our office. You never know. You might get in.

(unsigned)

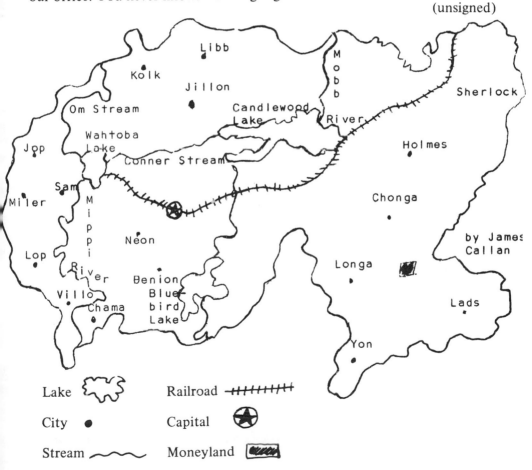

27

RAPER'S ISLAND

Legend

Volcanoes

Deadly Rivers

Trees

Shacks and Houses

Plains

Beaches

Population:

10 men
two million women

Island is
10 square miles big

Bikini Beach and Gulf

Strippers' Square

Rapers' Village

Smoochers' Beach Shack

This is an island of sexy girls strippers and Rapers. The boys have fun all day and night (in bed!) with a girl.

(unsigned)

Religion

Nearly all the kids have written travel pieces—many of them wonderful—but their imaginary worlds as yet lack definition, flesh, substance. I wanted to come up with an assignment which would help the kids focus more directly on their worlds. And I was interested, too, in suggesting something that might give them a chance to approach some of the larger questions I believe they have already planted beneath the surface of their writing. For example, are their worlds dreamlike, or nightmarish, are they in a place that's truly good, or truly evil?

Therefore—no it couldn't really have been therefore—today's assignment: to write about a religious ceremony in an imaginary place. I hoped that in so doing the kids might create objects of worship which would embody the essential nature of their imaginary worlds—and stand as useful symbols for their later writing. As an introduction to the idea, I plan to read a slightly condensed version of the Solidarity Day Ceremony from Huxley's *Brave New World,* the passage which ends with the chant:

> Orgy Porgy, Ford and Fun
> Kiss the girls and make them one.

Marv has questioned the assignment. Too great a leap into the abstract, too intellectual, likely to confuse or even offend the kids in the class who are religious—if I understand his criticism. I reply that my real interest is in ceremony, action, movement and celebration, not in intellectualizing the question of religion. But now, writing after the fact, I realize that my goals may may have been in conflict. On the one hand I wanted the kids to continue to write their spontaneous fantasies, on the other I wanted to develop some of the larger issues of Utopian and Dystopian writing. This conflict within me may have caused much of the problem.

Discussion begins. Miss Kintisch asks about the religions they have studied. Christianity, Buddhism, Islam. Names. Something a little more concrete about an African sect which worships a snake, then sacrifices one of its members to the snake each year. She asks the kids whether this is a good or bad religion. The kids say bad, of course. They are sullen; the discussion is flat, deadly. I begin: how about an imaginary religion. "You could worship trees, animals." Nothing very striking in their responses. I ask about Greek and Roman myths. To my surprise, the kids say they have never studied them. So I mention gods of war, or love, the seasons, fire. Timmy Adams, a small but tough looking kid with long floppy blond hair, suddenly lets loose with an incredible diatribe against religion. "It's just a way of controlling people," he says. Wow! The first sign of life today.

I agree that this is often true of states which have one official religion. I mention *1984* as an example of a state in which religion as we know it is prohibited. But with an official substitute—Big Brother—who may or may not exist. But aside from Timmy's outburst, nothing is happening. I feel like I'm treading water.

So I decide to read the Huxley piece—it seems much more concrete than anything we've discussed, or are going to discuss, today. I try to give some needed background to the piece first, mentioning the assembly-line babies, the use of drugs. Our Ford, and the gossip about Bernard's birth (to explain why he is not exactly comfortable with these ceremonies). It is a difficult passage, the kids may not understand all of it, but, for the most part, I get the feeling they are interested, attracted by its strangeness if nothing else. Then I ask the kids if they would like to write. "Suppose you're back in your imaginary world, you come upon a group of people. Maybe at first you don't understand what they're doing. Then you realize you're watching a religious celebration."

Most of the kids do write, perhaps they are just relieved to get away from the discussion. There are a number of whimsical, cute pieces (pizza worship, T.V. worship) suggesting little involvement in the assignment. Most disappointing, there is hardly any connection between what the kids write today and their previous work.

Conclusions. Ugh. There are so many different factors to be weighed. Certainly the mood of the discussion didn't help. Possibly the assignment was too intellectual, and did go over the heads of the kids. I just don't know. I am certain that I handled my part of the discussion badly—giving far too much attention to "what is it possible to worship" type questions, and not enough to celebration and movement. Perhaps the idea would have worked better without any preliminary discussion at all, and perhaps it is too much to expect any continuity after my long absence.

Incidentally, Timmy wrote, in part: "I think religion is and was just a way of controlling people. When I say there isn't any god I feel guilty like I'll get struck in the head with a bolt of lightning."

P.S. A few days later, while observing a class at 70, I noticed the following on the board: Homework Assignment # 7: Compare our religions of today with the religion of the Egyptians. My god! in one night? There is much to be considered when relating writing ideas to the regular schoolwork of the kids.

TWO FROM THE SIXTH GRADE:

GOD (T.V.) Worship

We sit in front of our color or black and white god, not caring if it gave us headaches or radiation destroy our eyes and wear Beanie caps that have antennae sticking out of it and fight to get to watch what we want on its wondrous screen!

There is also someone who we worship also. He is the man that sacrifices his tubes and transistors to our god. He also removes dirt from our god.

The way our god punishes us is to have a whole week of soap operas so we can't watch.

Jason Brill

To worship
use it on paper and
make straight lines.

David Bernhardt

I am anxious to see what happens with the religious ceremony idea with the older kids. The eighth grade class is loose and relaxed today, and there is noise throughout the period. We decide it's too much trouble to form a circle and I try to talk loudly with a limited degree of success. The greatest difference between the two classes is that, here, the discussion is underplayed—it's casual, even pretty confused at times—while in the sixth grade class it was overdirected, overcontrolled, and simply done to death.

The kids are enthusiastic and we soon develop an interesting list of possible objects of worship, including money, nature, power and love. I find myself talking more about books than usual. I mention *Ape and Essence* (devil worship) and *1984* in addition to *Brave New World*. Then we begin writing.

An astonishing number of kids write and the few who don't are busy drawing. I circulate around the room, mostly just talking to the kids, since little encouragement seems necessary.

The writing is interesting and varied. There are a number of "Death Religion" pieces (girls write these, too). Some are accompanied by beautifully executed and particularly gruesome drawings directly influenced by the comics (i.e.: a raised sword dripping blood, with the caption "Die!!!" A monster melting into a jelly-like mass "No!!! Ahh!!! Arhhah!!!")

But there are love religions, and comic initiation rites as well: "Next you will be escorted to the *Pit*. They have laid out tamales with red pepper sauce on top, and horse radish sprinkles. You must take the whole bowl into your mouth without wincing, then hold it while digging the pit one foot deeper, then swallow with a smile."

Colin Klebanoff's is my favorite. It is very short, very precise in its details, and the perfect ceremony for the Joint Chiefs of Staff: "In the middle of the huge hall, the group of 13 women and 12 men stood in their blue and red robes, singing and meditating they looked down at the table that they had gathered around, the antique marble that had survived from 1980 and now was still intact, 4 centuries later. Then the preacher of the group stood and said, 'Peace is the way, it has brought us to the time of paradise.' Then

32

the band started toward the door. As they left they bowed to the statue of their god, which was only two years younger than the marble table. It was an inactive atom bomb."

So, the idea here was at least partially successful. My questions about it remain unanswered, however. Is it the difference in the age of the kids that is crucial, or the differences in the way the idea was presented??

EIGHTH GRADE EXAMPLES:

THE EVIL ELKS

The ELKS are a secret religion who believe in complete Evil. They praise Evil and do all Evil.

To get in this religion, first you must cut the eye pupil out of your left eye and keep it in an alcohol jar in the ELK temple. And to be a leader you must cut off your right index finger.

The ELKS tattoo a bloody dagger across their face. The dagger is a symbol of the ELKS and no ELKS can leave the temple without a dagger pack on their arm.

The ELKS stay in packs wherever they go. So if anything ever happens they can make it worse. They will kill anyone or thing that gets in their way They have no cares or fears.

ELKS live only for a few months after they join because soon after the left eye goes blind, the other one will go a few months later.

As soon as an ELK is completely blind he drenches himself with gas and lights himself up. Then he becomes an ELK saint.

Wayne Teagaren

This is what will happen
if they let George Wallace
win the Presidency!

CHURCH OF WALLACISM

Be seated

Sermon: The lord Giveth thee your white soul which has the blessed fruit of all mankind. A soul which is gaveth beyond equality with different colored souls. For the lord giveth thy gift upon us.

The lord be with you.

People: And with your spirit. Amen.

Sermon: Thee spirit must be holy for thou spirit must reach thy brave-
ness and loyalness towards the white man and teach purity until thou is blessed by the Ku Klux Klan.

> We praise the lord
> head of the Ku Klux Klan

People: Amen, God be with you.

Sermon: And with your spirit.

Sermon: Town News—Slaying of three black children will take place
in front of church. Be on hand for the amusement.

Fred Zydel

AN IMAGINARY RELIGION

As we entered the world for the third time the grassy streets of this
beautiful world were empty. We walked on and on. Then around a large grassy hill all the people of the world were dancing around. As we came closer
we saw that they were dancing around a big stone statue. On the top of the
statue were the letters L, O, V, E.

Since this seemed the kind of religion we believed in we too started
dancing around. After a couple of hours of worshipping this statue, everyone
went home and brought back food. There were meats, vegetables, corn, tur-
keys and many different kinds of foods. Then everyone sat down and ate and
ate and *ate*. After everyone ate they all talked and loved and did all sorts of
things. We found the man who had been our guide and asked him how long
the people did this. He said they did it every afternoon of every day. We
thought this was fantastic but excused ourselves because we had to go. And
we went, but promised we would return.

Lisa Methfessal

Continuity in Writing

The similarity between this class and the sixth graders whom I have just left really surprises me. I had come to expect a certain holding back, a certain skepticism, from this class. Instead, from the moment I distribute their work, there is the same enthusiasm, the same frantic flipping of pages—even the same determination to read the work of their classmates. And we have a wonderful reading. The one new problem which I encounter, however — and one that I have been expecting—is the question of continuity. After the reading, when I ask the kids if they'd like to continue their stories, three of four of them declare, "But I'm finished." And it's true.

In both my classes I have noticed how kids will rush to complete a piece, often tacking on lines in the last few minutes before the bell which have little or nothing to do with what they've been writing. Nearly all the writing that they are asked to do in school is so neatly circumscribed, there are no open-ended projects, and I believe these kids feel they are actually *expected* to write pat beginnings and endings. The eighth graders are particularly adept—they seem to know exactly how much time is left in a period, and exactly how much writing will win the approval of their teachers—which is why I meet this problem here for the first time. I've tried to recall my own writing experiences in school, and I am quite certain that I was never asked to do any "creative" writing that occupied more than a single classroom period, was of course asked for longer work, but these were always expository pieces—essays, term papers, etc.

I've debated walking into a classroom without saying a word, and writing TO BE CONTINUED in huge block letters across the board. But I don't think this is a solution since kids (not only kids) frequently write themselves into dead ends. When this happens, you simply must turn around and begin again. But is it possible to distinguish between a legitimate dead end and a convenient one? I mean the stories which break off abruptly with lines like "then I woke up," or "but it was all a dream." I may as well admit that I have been mightily tempted to delete final sentences like these when I'm reproducing the kids' works. Or, as an alternative, I might just write in the margins. "No, you didn't wake up. This is no dream!" But that's just too manipulative, and a real danger to the work I want to accomplish.

I've obviously invested heavily in the idea of encouraging kids to work on longer pieces. Therefore, I must remind myself constantly that this simply cannot be forced. I have always tried to leave an "out" for the kids. If they don't like the assignment they can write something else. I realize the same "out" is needed when it comes to questions of continuity. So I tell the kids that I'd like them to continue their stories if possible, and that nothing they write for me has to have a regular beginning or ending as far as I'm concerned. But if they're really finished, or stuck, or just tired of what they've already written, then they can write anything else they want.

Perhaps this is no solution. Perhaps all it really amounts to is waiting to see what happens. But I think waiting is important, and that the kids must find an idea that they themselves really want to pursue. I hope the theme of Utopias is really large enough and varied enough for them to discover possibilities which they consider worthy of extended development.

In any case, it is a very productive class. Once again, distributing the kids' work seems to have the greatest effect on the least secure kids. And the "stars" write little, with one notable exception. Lisa Methfessal, who wrote a wonderful piece about bicycling under the Hudson River (and nearly getting caught in the seaweed) to get to her imaginary world. She continues without a moment's hesitation. "On my second visit . . . " she begins.

War

I feel that I'm overflowing with ideas, though really I have only three. The first came from a long conversation with Miguel Ortiz, in which we began to reminisce about our own elementary school days. Miguel confessed to a childhood obsession with battle plans. He found them in an encyclopedia, studied them carefully, then re-enacted each battle with toy soldiers and blocks. From the moment he mentioned it, I knew I had an idea I wanted to try in my classes: to conceive of a war in an imaginary land, a war unlike any we have ever known. I was struck by the fact that here was an assignment which could be realized visually (the kids could simply draw elaborate battle plans of their own), or through writing, or through a combination of the two. Finally, it allowed for a full range of responses. An imaginary war, after all, might be joyful, or outrageously comic, or it could be terrible, cruel and brutal.

I headed for the library that evening. Here I had a minor disappointment. The plans I found (in the Encyclopedia Britannica) were very small and hardly what you could call elaborate. But I copied them anyway. They looked like this:

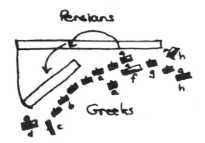

a. Right of Phalanx   e. Hypaspists
b. Left of Phalanx   f. Heavy Cavalry
c. Light Infantry   g. Light Infantry
d. Cavalry   h. Light Cavalry

Battle of Arabela, or Guagamela, (331 B.C.), Showing tactics of rear attack.

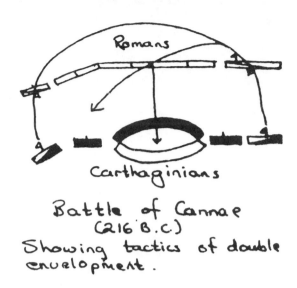

Battle of Cannae
(216 B.C.)
Showing tactics of double
envelopment.

Sheila looked at the plans. Undaunted, she found some shelf paper and magic markers, and reproduced them as wall charts, five or six feet long with marvelous colors. I was overjoyed.

Second idea: an imaginary war requires imaginary weapons. Here the work has been done for me. Dick Gallup devised a marvelous gun assignment last year. He asked his kids to invent a new kind of gun, and they responded with a series of fantastic, mostly benevolent, weapons. We printed many of them in a recent newsletter, and I brought copies along to show my kids.

Third, I had been looking over Kurt Vonnegut's work for possible use in the classroom. In *Slaughterhouse-Five*, I discovered a wonderful war scene —an imaginary war. Billy Pilgrim sits down in front of his television set and becomes "Slightly unstuck in time." He watches a World War II Air Force movie. It runs backwards. It is a wonderful passage:

> American planes, full of holes and wounded men and corpses took off backwards from an airfield in England. Over France, a few German fighter planes flew at them backwards, sucked bullets and shell fragments from some of the planes and crewmen. They did the same for wrecked American bombers on the ground, and those planes flew up backwards to join the formation.
>
> The formation flew backwards over a German city that was in flames. The bombers opened their bomb bay doors, exerted a miraculous magneticism which shrunk the fires, gathered them into cylindrical steel containers, and lifted the containers into the bellies of the planes. The containers were stored neatly in racks. The Germans below had miraculous devices of their own, which were long steel tubes. They used them to suck more fragments from the crewmen and planes. But there were still a few wounded Americans, though, and some of the bombers were in bad repair. Over France, though, German fighters came up again, made everything and everybody as good as new.

When the bombers got back to their base, the steel cylinders were taken from the racks and shipped back to the United States of America, where factories were operating day and night, dismantling the cylinders, separating the dangerous contents into minerals. Touchingly, it was mainly women who did this work. The minerals were then shipped to specialists in remote areas. It was their business to put them into the ground, to hide them cleverly, so they would never hurt anybody again.

The American fliers turned in their uniforms, became high school kids.

I asked the kids if they knew what the wall charts represented. They guessed battles almost immediately. The boys were tremendously excited. They wanted to know exactly what happened in each battle. I told them that I really didn't understand battle plans very well, in fact, that I'd never looked at one until yesterday, and that I had very little interest in the subject. But I said I would try to tell them what I had learned from the encyclopedia. I cleared my throat loudly and began my explanation with my deepest most serious voice. (I felt like Nixon explaining our recent successes in Laos and Cambodia.)

I don't remember exactly what I said, something like: Alexander the Great concentrated his troops here, broke through the Persian lines here, then attacked from the rear. The encyclopedia says it's a classic example of rear attack. Very important to study if you want to learn how to shoot people in the back.

   or

Here are the names for Alexander's troops: light infantry, cavalry, etc. I couldn't find any names for the Persians. Maybe they don't get any names because they are lost.

Pretty bad jokes. But the kids were laughing and I was really having a great time. The boys pressed me for more information. They were already comparing the two battles and saying which was their favorite. But I was beginning to lose the girls, so I decided it was time for some imaginary guns. I read the example in the newsletter: "This is a gun that shoots candy to children in the world. I eat the candy too." And suddenly I felt the class was complete, that the kids now realized that this didn't have to be a real battle, that their imaginary world armies could come together to do happy, joyful, loving things if they wanted. I read a few more of Gallup's guns, which the kids really enjoy.

A number of guns appear—a real tribute, I think, to Gallup's assignment —and there are a few interesting pieces of writing. Randy Besman begins a wonderful battle between the Slobs and the Neatlings, complete with a battle diagram. Victoria Larkin somehow manages to continue her story "The Doll." And Ann Turner begins a wonderful war in which the armies first throw flowers, then charge and tickle one another. But these are all just beginnings.

SIXTH GRADE PIECES:

I was going swimming on a hot summer day by myself. When I got there I dived in. I saw something shining by the drain. I swam to it and I got sucked in. I fell down and hit land. There was air there. I was walking for a mile or two when peas were shooting all over the air. One hit me and it got squashed. Another one came but I ducked and it didn't hit me on the ground. I looked around and I saw little green men shooting peas. I was so startled I just jumped. Then one of the green men looked at me and said "we're not really green —it's just that the enemy shot peas all over us and we turned green." When I calmed down I told him how I got here and said I wanted to get back up the drain. He said if I helped him, he would get me back. So I agreed to help. He told me if I stopped the war, that's when he would. I went over to the people who were fighting and asked them if they would stop, but one of them shot me in the mouth. I spit it out and took all the guns away from them. They all shouted at me and they tried to pull me down but they weren't strong enough to. I ran over to the other army and took their guns away too. Then I pushed them all together and said to stop fighting. They all agreed. Then I asked the man and he brought me back up the drain. I was going to tell my mother, but she wouldn't believe me.

The End

Eric Wolf

One morning during my stay in the city I woke up and heard extra excitement and bustling on the streets.

I got up and went to the window. When I looked out I saw old women preparing a big feast and setting up beautiful decorations all along the streets.

Then I stuck my head out of my window and looked at a very large group of small children. They were coming from the meadow; each had a large basket of fresh-picked daisies.

So, full of excitement and curiosity, I got dressed and ran outside without breakfast. When I got there I asked what it was all about. The ladies looked at me in astonishment and said, "Why of course today is the day of the tournament between the east side of town and the west.

And with that she handed me a basket of daisies and said, "Now go over there and join the rest of the young people."

I wandered over there and saw that all of the little children I saw before were handing over these flowers to the other people around me. Then I recognized a friend in the crowd. He said "Just watch me and do what I do."

Then he led me over to a kind of terrace. I looked across—there were other kids also with flowers.

Just then the east side charged out from under the terrace and everyone started throwing daisies on them, so I did too.

Then before I knew what happened, someone grabbed me from behind and started tickling me; being the ticklish sort I started to laugh hysterically.

Then I was dragged to the main street of town where a feast was waiting. For some reason I started laughing along with everyone.

Ann Turner

. . . And out of the grayness came what I think is a native of this universe, so I asked him where we were in the middle of the war of the Slobs and the Neatlings. . . he continued to say the slobs threw all of their Garbage out of their guns and the Neatlings threw white dust out of theirs, and then splat—right in the eye.

You see the slobs shot slop because the Neatlings couldn't stand anything sloppy. But the Neatlings shot white dust, because they wanted to make the slobs happy. Then the little man said he was supposed to be my escort to see general Ianschtineshvine about my clothes. The general was looking just like a pale snowflake—he had medals down to his waist, he had high white leather boots and long white bell-bottoms with a white leather jacket and vest, with a white velvet bellsleeved shirt. He talked in a very low voice. He said "I want to talk to you about that shirt of yours"—(then he yelled) and said, "I could have you arrested for wearing such a ghastly garment."

"But since you're new here, I won't." So I said, "What's wrong with my clothes?" "Well," he said, "There is a brown speck of dirt on your garment." "Oh that's just a speck of dirt—here, I'll brush it off onto the floor," I said. "No you don't. I don't want that piece of unsanitary speck of bacteria contaminating my office! Dump your debris in the debris eliminator," said the general. "All right," I said. So I put it in and I heard some pretty strange noises. First I heard violins, then a humming sound.

Randy Besman

A few weeks later, I gave the Imaginary War assignment to my eighth grade class. I was a little worried that the kids might find this idea too childish, but if anything, they were more responsive than the sixth graders. Jose's story is perhaps the most amazing, for it is not just an imaginary war, but a war within a war.

AN IMAGINARY BATTLE

That's about the tenth time they've come close. If I'm not careful I may not live to daydream. I'm thinking of a place where you can get shot without

41

getting wounded or killed. It's on a far-off planet in the next to nearest galaxy. On this planet there are many wars, for the poeple are always arguing about something or other. But unlike the wars on Earth, where they pump you full of lead, the weapons here are suspended animation guns. When the ray hits you, you go into a deep sleep for a year or two. Never aging or changing physically or mentally. This is good because nobody gets hurt. You awaken when the war is over. Thus, the battle is over quickly. There is no physical combat. All fighting is done with suspended animation guns.

I didn't want to come to this place of death, but I was forced with the security of my family. I wish I was on that planet where you can't get shot. I'd better keep down, they're coming closer.

Jose

TWO OTHER EIGHTH GRADE PIECES:

AN IMAGINARY WAR

Down, Down. Down. We are going for the 4th time back to the imaginary world. It was April 24th, 1972, and again we were back in the beautiful world. As we entered the streets were empty. We thought they were worshipping their god but when we got to the place of worship no one was there. We decided to take a walk for a while until the people came back. After an hour we heard music over the hill and we all ran that way. 600 of the men in the city were all shooting about 40 people. But as we got closer we saw that the 600 or so men were shooting the 40 people with music guns and chicklet cannons with gum drop cannon balls and heart-shaped guns that shoot beautiful light on the people. After the love war was over we asked what the people that were being shot at felt like and an old man with a smile on his face said, "The other day I was mean to everyone, but after I got shot I seemed warmer and wanted to love everyone around." We smiled at him and said good-bye. So we journeyed back home and thought of all the beautiful things we learned in this imaginary world.

Lisa Methfessel

BATTLE OF THE PLANTS

Once I went to Prof. Brainiacs office to speak to him about a medicine he prescribed for me. He told me he gave me the right prescription. By mistake he gave me a solution-like thing that made me smaller and smaller. I was so small I went right through a hole in the ground.

I found myself among the roots of the roses in the rose garden. Then I spotted a root that looked very different. It was the roots of a weed. I thought, "If this weed sucks up all the water from this soil the roses will die." All of a sudden the soil was getting wet. I thought it must be raining. I saw the roses were trying to get some water but the weed roots were sucking it all up.

There was a great battle between the roses and the weed. Although there was only one weed and a number of roses, the weed was much stronger.

Each time the flowers tried to get water the weed's roots would invade them and suck the water right to its main stem.

I stood there and stared. At the same moment all the roots of the roses came together. All at once they sucked up all the fresh water from the roots of the weed.

The battle was over! The flowers were pretty and were full of fresh water. But, of course, the weed died off without any food but the sun and the air.

To my amazement, I felt the ground packing up on me. No, I was wrong I was growing back to my regular size.

Sara Morales

I decided to devote one more session to Imaginary Wars. The kids seemed to be having great fun with it, but had had little real time for writing last week. Quite unexpectedly, this session became one of the most important of the year for me—for it led me to consider a whole new approach to teaching.

It all began with my search for some new way to get back into the assignment. I spent a very long night looking for new material on wars in an imaginary place, but could find nothing as powerful or exciting as the Vonnegut piece which I had already used. Finally, about two A.M., with a sudden burst of energy, I decided to write my own imaginary war to read to the kids. In it I used one of Carmen's weapons (a gun that turns you invisible) to show more concretely how an imaginary weapon could be used in the heat of combat. I started the class by telling the kids that it really wasn't fair to ask them to write all the time without ever writing myself. I said that one of Carmen's guns had given me the idea for my story and that I would like to read it. Simple as that.

The kids' response was fantastic. It really didn't matter to them whether the story was a good one or not. What was important was that I had written something, anything. The moment I stopped reading the kids asked, "can we give you writing assignments?" I was delighted and said I thought that was a great idea. We talked about this for a while, but of course the kids found it difficult to come up with assignments for me off the tops of their heads. So I promised that the next time I came in we would sit down together and think of lots of writing ideas. Then they could choose something for themselves that they would like to write about, and assign one idea to me.

Everyone agreed that this was a good way to work, and I was terribly excited. I couldn't have planned a more meaningful change from the way I had been working. It seemed a perfectly timed solution to the questions I had been asking about uniform assignments.

I was particularly worried about the effect such assignments were having on some of the more self-reliant kids. I had become fairly certain that this approach interfered with the directions these children would have followed naturally in their writing if there hadn't been the pressure to conform to a a single idea. Victoria Larkin's work is a good example. During my first visit she wrote a truly extraordinary story, "The Doll." She was absent during some of the later sessions but was present for the initial discussion of the Imaginary War idea. She responded to the assignment, rather dutifully, and even ingeniously, I think, somehow working a war into the context of her story. Even so, the pieces just didn't seem to fit together, and I wonder where the story might have gone without my interference.

I am still stranded in space with that stupid doll, Rachel. Oh by the way, my name is Vicky Larkin, in case you didn't know.

Oh well, I've decided that living (if that's what you want to call it) with Rachel is not to be continued, so I am going to throw her out into space.

One week later. . . . . This is the queerest planet I've ever seen. (That's funny—I've never seen any planets before.)

Finally someone is coming to greet me.

Oh crud, she sticks to me like that "rub & glue" junk (excuse me, but that's Rachel).

One week later. . . . . Guess what, Rachel started a war with another planet and she has decided to use my wisdom to win it. Well this is the battle plan. . . . .

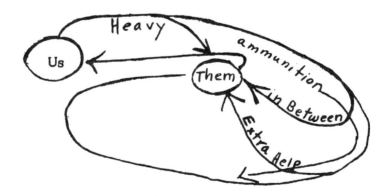

Four weeks later. . . The war is going good; so far no one has attacked, correction, some one just attacked me, Rachel's servant, obviously I goofed.

I goofed all right and boy did I ever! You should see the mess out there, I've never seen anything like it in my whole life (but then, I never wanted to or had the chance).

I really wish that there was something that I could do to make someone believe that Rachel is a doll! I mean look (well anyway read) how would you feel if you lived in a perfectly peaceful nation (which of course you don't) how would you feel if someone came into your world and made you believe that they were a god, then they totally took over, started a war, and there was nothing you could do about it. Well, that's the spot I'm in, but to make someone believe me about her being a doll I could always break her, or un-stuff her (if she's stuffed, which I don't know cause I didn't have her long enough to figure that out).

I'd better quit for the moment, because here she comes.

Victoria Larkin

Toward a Variety of Topics

Today was a day of learning for me and, quite possibly, my best day ever in a classroom. There had been an unexpected snowfall during the early hours of the morning. The city had not yet managed to turn it into the usual gray mush, and even Ninth Avenue looked clean and lovely as I walked to school feeling quite exhilarated. I had deliberately tried to avoid thinking about the class—about my expectations for it, that is—which amounted to something of a task for me. But I was determined to leave the day open.

There was a great feeling in the class, too. The kids needed no reminder about our plans for today, particularly that part which involved their giving me a writing assignment. They formed a circle in the front of the room (standard procedure by now) while I began the class by listing all the topics that we had written about so far on the board. Then I asked for new ideas. Our list grew very quickly: plants, animals, weather, schools, sports, food, laws (wow! this was Randy Besman's idea). Most of the ideas stood by themselves and I simply wrote them on the board without further discussion. Some we talked about in more detail. For example, when someone mentioned weather we looked out at the snow and talked about other things that might fall from the sky ("money, chemicals"). And I was delighted when Denise suggested animals, because I had brought a newsletter with me that contained Dick Gallup's "bestiary," with some wonderful examples of imaginary animals created by sixth graders at P.S. 20. I read a few of these and then passed the newsletter around to those kids who were interested.

Finally, since so much time remained in the period, I added one item of my own to the list. I had been looking over Bruno Bettelheim's *The Children of the Dream* with the hope of finding some concrete description of communal child rearing and kibbutz life. I could not find such a passage—most of descriptive material was difficult and not appropriate for reading out loud to the children —so I simply mentioned some of the general aspects of kibbutz living. I said that, in an average kibbutz, a child's "family" is the entire community, though a child's real parents are part of this community. I said that all the children of the kibbutz were raised together in the dormitories, and contrasted this to the idea of "home" and "family" that we grow up with. At the bottom of the list I wrote "family" with a big question mark and suggested that someone might like to write about a world in which children are raised differently—without families, perhaps not in communes or kibbutzas either—but in some new way. I added only that this was a pretty difficult idea, and that I would need lots of time to think about it before writing.

Our list completed, I ask the kids for my assignment. Immediate consensus, they want me to write about an imaginary school. Ok.

We begin writing. Originally, I had wanted to write with the kids, but there was still lots to do. I had a set of the kids' writing from a previous session, not yet reproduced, which I spread out on a counter in the back of the room. I told the kids they could come back and refer to it if they wanted, and many did. Most of the kids chose to work on imaginary animals, perhaps because this idea involved drawing as well as writing. But there were a few weather pieces as well, and Randy was hard at work drafting laws for his world of the Slobs and Neatlings. There were also many words to spell, and many questions, so I gave up on the idea of writing and told the kids I would do the assignment as homework.

I felt very good about the class. I don't know, perhaps it was less productive than some of the other sessions. But we've all trapped ourselves into believing that a thick packet of papers at the end of a class is a sure criterion of success. I no longer believe this and, anyway, I think something more important may have happened today, and that is that these kids are beginning to find their own ways of relating to the imaginary worlds theme.

Ann

It was not until after the class that I discovered that something extraordinary had happened. Ann Turner had responded to the family/kibbutz discussion and started a story in which she imagines she is sixteen, is leaving her parents for the first time, and is about to take up residence in an ancestral home "used for all the girls in my family." I had never seen writing like this from a sixth grader—her story maintained a delicate balance between the real and the imaginary that reminded me of Shirley Jackson's "The Lottery." There is the same attention to concrete, familiar detail (she eats an apple, combs her hair, puts on her good slippers) within an undefinable, vaguely disturbing setting. ("We lined up in the center of the square. Then the elders walked up to us.") I was amazed. Moreover, Ann told me that she wants to continue working on it.

It was fortunate that a few weeks after this I began working with a smaller group of sixth graders. I continued to follow a regular schedule of weekly visits, would poke my nose into the geography class, and about seven or eight kids, including Ann, would come running out. We would search for a vacant room on the floor, and begin our work there.

For the first time I had the opportunity to reach the kids on a more intimate basis. As a result, I was able to follow Ann's story closely, to offer praise, encouragement and criticism when needed. Ann never wavered in her determination to write her story. Often, I would begin group writing activities with four or five of the other kids. There would be lots of noise, talk and laughter. But Ann was seldom distracted. She would sit in back of the room writing, away from the rest of us. Sometimes she and Vicky and Dina (who were also writing stories) would sit together. They would talk, pass their stories back and forth, giggle and gossip. I was always sure that no writing would get done. But, by the end of class, Ann always had a new page.

TWO ANECDOTES:

Ann is used to being a good student, expects praise, is possibly even a little spoiled by it. During my first visit to the school I noticed that she would raise her hand in response to almost every question and, if not called on, would sigh and slump in her seat with a look of total anguish. I was not too surprised, then, when one day after class I told her that her story was really very good, she smiled, coyly averted her eyes, and said only. . . "I know."

At the end of a later session, Ann told me that she was at loose ends and didn't know what to write next. I took her story home, re-read it carefully, and wrote her a one-page letter, again praising the work, then suggesting three or four directions for further development based on themes or characters she had introduced in the story but not yet resolved (i.e., What happens to Magie? Do you see her again? — etc.). Ann read the letter at the beginning of the next class, we talked awhile, and then she told me that she now knew how to go on. She continued as before (actually, she had taken two of the suggestions and combined them in her own way) and I soon forgot about the letter. About three weeks later, I noticed that she had purchased a notebook that she was using just for story-writing. Inside the notebook, which she carried everywhere with her, was the letter, looking very battered and used. I was quite moved.

The lesson I learned from Ann's work was a profound one, and I want to try to state it with some degree of precision. When I first started this project, I believed that children might be encouraged to write longer works through a clever ordering of discrete topics all related to the imaginary worlds theme. That is, I thought that children might first write about traveling to an imaginary place, then perhaps about how the place looked and felt, then about one or more of its institutions. Eventually, I hoped the kids would merge these discrete topics into a single Utopian or Dystopian vision.

I learned from Ann to look at the topics in a much different way. I see them now as a useful beginning—a way of introducing the imaginary worlds theme to children in a manner which is not overwhelming, which the kids seem to enjoy, and which allows them to begin writing immediately. After that, it is necessary to be more flexible, to open up a variety of topics, and to find areas that the kids themselves want to pursue, The key to larger works, I'm now convinced, must be found in each child's own writing or conversation—not in a list of topics. In Ann's story, as it subsequently developed, a feeling for the Architecture, the Landscape, the Role of the Elders in her world are all present; but they are all subordinate to the dramatic events portrayed in her story, and are certainly not the primary reason for writing it.

Once I had the opportunity to work on a more intimate level with children, this change in my approach came almost automatically and instinctively. Once I had seen the first page of Ann' story, I knew how absurd it would have been to suggest "now, why not write something about imaginary architecture." The story had to be approached on its own terms. True, not all children's work is as startling as Ann's, nor are all children as self-directed; so a topics list, and possibly a set of literary examples to help define each idea, will be useful for varying periods of time with different children. But I know that my own work would have been far better had I stopped depending on the topics a little earlier. The great enemy was time and the circumstances which forced me to work before a whole class, in the traditional role of teacher.

ANN'S STORY

Chapter I

Today was the day. Today I was sixteen. First I would have a big feast and then go to the small stone house my great great great grandfather had built for my great great grandmother (his daughter).

It had been used for all the girls in my family.

Mother is still moving around the house packing the last of my clothes.

I am in the kitchen eating an apple. I wonder if I really will make it all by myself. The girl next door didn't. She had to come back.

But I think I will. I have a job with Mr. Westberg making lace, and I know pretty much how to take care of myself. Besides, Mom and Dad think I'm ready.

I ran upstairs and put my good slippers on and combed out my hair and put my ribbons on and ran outside.

There was the most beautiful feast waiting for me. I had seen the feast before when older children had gone, but it never felt like this before.

I went over to where my friends were all in a group. They seemed as nervous as I am. Just then the whistle blew. We lined up in the center of the square. Then the elders walked up to us. They said the traditional speech about how it would be on our own.

Afterwards my great grandmother came over to me. "Be careful," she said. "You are going through the most important part in your entire life."

I started trembling. "Of course I'll make it," I assured myself. "Why not? My mother and grandmother did."

I felt a tug at my arm. I looked up and there was my friend. "Come on," she said, "we will miss the dance."

We got in our places and before I knew it my body started dancing the dance I knew by heart.

After the dance we walked over and got refreshments.

It was a wonderful day full of excitement and fun.

At last the evening came. We were all very tired. I walked home and got my bags. There was Mom and Dad and little brother. Dad handed me my bags and Mom kissed me and cried a little bit.

"Good bye," they said in harmony. Even my brother felt sad.

I walked to the corner and there was Magie. Her new home was right next to mine. For many years to come it was going to be "My Home," I said aloud. It sounded funny.

"What took you so long?" Magie shouted. I started to run toward her. When I got there we started walking in the direction of our new homes. The village was quiet except for a few kids or rather grownups who were still celebrating. But we were too tired for that.

"Good night," I said to Magie.

"Good night," she said. "See you tomorrow."

With that I walked up and turned on the porch light. I walked in; what a mess! There was an inch of dust all over,—"I have to clean this up in the morning," I thought to myself. "I'm too tired now."

With that I went to the back room and went to bed. I didn't care how it looked. And the next moment I was asleep.

Chapter II

In the morning I woke to see the sun shining in the house. This house was cheerful!

I got up and immediately got dressed and started cleaning. To my a-mazement the water pipes were still working. I spent the rest of the morning cleaning and pretty soon the house started to shape up. Then I decided to take a shower.

After I got cleaned up I started to go to town to get some food. I was starving!

As I started to go out the door I saw Gregory.

"Can I borrow two eggs?" he said. I was a little surprised but I said, "I was just going to the store now. Would you like to come?"

"O.K." he replied. And with that we started off.

When we were coming back with the food Magie stopped me and said, "Can I talk to you for a minute?"

"Sure," I said. "See you later, Greg."

"Come on in."

We walked over to the kitchen table. "Sit down," I said. "I just have to put away these few things."

When I was through I sat down next to her. "What's the matter?" I said.

"I've been thinking," she started. "We're really all alone. What I mean is we're on our own and frankly I've been feeling very nervous."

"Listen," I said. "Why don't you stay here tonight?"

"All right."

"Hey," I said. "How about some eggs? I bet you're starving."

"Yeh," she said.

We ate them quickly and then I said "how about going down to the field to pick blueberries? Like we did when we were little?"

"O.K. by me," Magie said.

We went down to the field and picked all afternoon. We picked about 10 baskets but ate at least 5.

Everything was so carefree I felt like a babe again.

At last we decided it was time we had better start heading home. Evening was coming on. We headed for Magie's house first to pick up some clothes. Then we started back to my house. I fixed some spaghetti and Magie made the salad and with that we went to bed.

During the middle of the night I was awakened by a cry. I got up and there was Magie, hysterical at the foot of the bed.

"Ann," Magie said. "It's stupid. I can't go on like this. I'm too nervous. I have to go home."

"Magie, are you sure you want to?"

"I've no other choice."

"But do you realize what this means?"

"Yes, but I've got to."

I understand what you mean all right. I'll go with you to see your parents tomorrow."

"O.K."

"But try to get some sleep now."

"Good night."

It was a long night. I tossed and turned in my sleep. Magie was really going home. I always thought she was stronger than that.

In the morning we slowly walked into the village. "Poor Magie," I couldn't help thinking.

We finally got to her parents' door.

"Mom, Dad." Magie began. "I've got something to talk you to about."

"I'd better be going," I said, as I turned and walked away. I knew they would want to be alone.

After that I stopped being afraid of going home. I'd have to be stronger than Magie if I am to make it.

Chapter III

For the next week or so I saw a lot of Greg. He is in real lousy shape as far as housekeeping goes.

But I really think we have a lot going with each other.

"Ann, come with me to the other side of the forest."

On one side of the village was the sea, and about five miles on the other side was a forest that none have ventured beyond.

"Are you proposing?"

With a blush, "yes."

"I'd love to, but are you sure it's safe? When I was little my parents never even let me go into it."

"Don't worry. It's safe, and it's about time someone went through it."

While he was talking he slipped a ring onto my finger. I felt like something I never felt before.

All of a sudden his lips fell on mine.

I put my hand to my head. "Come on," I began with a huge smile and a little giggle. "We've got a lot to do."

I picked up his hand and we went into the village by bike.

First we went to my parents. I grabbed my mother's arm and pulled her into my ex-room to tell her. She gave me a smile, put her hand on mine, and said, "Tomorrow we will go pick out material for the dress."

"But I have to work tomorrow."

"Silly, we will do it in your lace shop. I'm sure Mr. Westberg won't mind."

"Of course."

In the distance I heard some mumbling. All I could hear was my father. I couldn't hear the words but he was talking in an advice tone, so when I joined Greg again I didn't ask what my father said.

The next day when I went into work the first thing Mr. Westberg said to me was, "Congratulations." Undoubtedly my mother had paid him a visit.

About 10:00 my mother came and we picked out some beautiful white silk.

That evening, Greg and I went to his house for dinner. He had already told his parents. When we walked in his papa put his arm around me and said, "Sweet Ann." I kissed him on the cheek, and a smile was exchanged between Greg and his mother. We went to dinner and basically it was a very pleasant evening. Greg walked me home and I brought up the subject of the forest.

"I've been thinking about transportation," Greg started. After we get through the forest we are going to need a vehicle, but it has to be one we can get through the forest."

"What about our bikes?"

"I don't know that they would be enough to hold all our supplies."

"Then, of course, a horse."

"I don't know. You see, that's our first problem. I'm sure we are going to face many others.

"We can talk about it in the morning. Goodnight."

The wedding was going to be on Friday and we were going to leave the the next morning. The ceremony was to be held in the little chapel and everyone in the village was going to be there. The week passed quickly until finally the day arrived. It was a beautiful spring wedding held exactly at noon. We went out to the square and I noticed that there was something under a sheet. The Mayor stepped up and pulled it off and there was the most beautiful sort of cart! I grabbed Greg's arm and said, "for us!"

"But how does it work?" asked Greg.

The Mayor took Greg and sat him in it. It was a wooden cart with two seats in the front and a big compartment in the back for storage and it had four big very flexible wheels.

"How does it go?" Greg examined the cart.

"You see those pedals? You both pedal them like the swan boat at the lake."

"Oh, wow."

"Let's take it for a trial run. Get in, Ann."

I hopped in and we rode around the square. It was a wonderful evening, with dancing and laughing. At last the merriment stopped and we went to bed.

Lisa

My greatest failure in the eighth grade class has been my inability to reach the kids individually. I simply haven't known how to go about it in a class of thirty. Lisa's latest work brings it all home to me. On my first visit, she wrote a wonderful piece about traveling on a bicycle under the Hudson River to her imaginary place. She has continued the same piece ever since, and it now has four or five long sections. Her imaginary world is a true Utopian vision, a place of love and peace, where all races and nationalities live happily together, where the cities glow and the sun is always shining.

When we wrote about religion, she wrote about a love-in. When we wrote about war, her armies shot candy and hearts and music. Her work has really been quite lovely, but when I re-read it in its entirety a few weeks ago, it seemed to be growing thin. What had started as a vision was becoming an exercise.

One problem seemed obvious, her writing merely played around the surface of the meaning of love, like the Beatles' "all you need is love." By doing so, she had of course raised a number of really profound issues, and I felt she might sustain her piece if she began to approach the deeper implications of her writing. There were so many issues I wanted to talk over with her. For example, did she really believe in her own world, how might it come about? How might children be raised, what sort of education might be devised to really promote love and brotherhood? Would some people still have irrational, destructive impulses? Can such impulses, if they exist, be rendered harmless by society? Does society have the right to render them harmless? And so on, and on. Naturally, I didn't intend to phrase the questions in this way, although everything I know about Lisa suggests that she could handle a

55

conversation of such complexity.

I have tried to talk with her before, during, and after classes, but there are always interruptions. All together, we have had perhaps five minutes of conversation. Last week, just before she ran off to another class, she told me that she thought her world was unreal. I asked why, isn't it possible to have a place where people really love one another. "No," she said, "there is always conflict." So she has run headlong into the Great Utopian Contradiction—a world made absolutely perfect is a world that can also be absolutely static and dull—but on a level far below her real capabilities. She is bored with her work and, God knows, a world that is a perpetual love-in, and nothing more, *is* boring. I don't blame her. I've done nothing to suggest a way out. And she is off to her next class before I can mumble something about how conflict might be made part of her world.

I realized today that the end was near, yet I felt completely trapped into giving another assignment to the class as a whole. Lisa wrote an interesting piece.

BACK AGAIN

The date is April 24, 1999. Again we decided to go back to the undersea world. As we entered the silver gates for the 4th time I saw someone and something I never saw before in this world. It was a man but he was black and beautiful. In all the time I've been in this world I never noticed anyone like him. Danny and Judy were eating so I went over to him and he immediately introduced himself. His name was Danky Neru. We started talking about where we came from and I found out he also came from the surface world we came from. After talking and eating and just enjoying each other for a while we took a walk. He told me he had been living on this world for 2 years and he couldn't take it anymore. I looked puzzled, then I asked him "why?"—it seemed like a beautiful world to me. He then replied, the more you come here the worse it gets, no one argues or disagrees, and no one loves each other individually. I then interrupted him, "that's right," I said. I finally noticed everyone loved each other but no one got together about it.

It was about 5 p.m. that night and we decided to go home, I knew I was in love with Danky Neru so I asked him if he wanted to go back with us. He looked at me and smiled and said, "When we get back let's do something together, O.K.?" I said yes and we were off.

Well here I am back home in New Port L.I. but Danky Neru isn't with me. You see he died as soon as we reached land. No one knows why. But I swore I would never go back to the undersea world. Because I know it killed the man called Danky Neru.

END

Lisa Methfessal

56

So, that's the end of that. I realize more than ever before how essential it is to approach kids individually if longer works are the aim, and I still don't know how it can be done in this situation. Uniform assignments are disastrous, except as openers, and even if I listed a hundred options on the board, I could never satisfy the needs of a student like Lisa. The only approach to this work that makes sense to me now is one that allows for individual encouragement, criticism, and specific suggestions to kids about how to continue.

Jeff

One day as I was leaving school after a session with the sixth graders, I met Jeff Weiss in the hall. He handed me two extraordinary imaginary world stories. Jeff was in the eighth grade, and was one of the kids that I would have wanted to include in a smaller writing group. As I said earlier, scheduling problems prevented this, and I felt (as a result) that my work with the eighth graders was really winding down. But for some reason, Jeff began working on his own stories independently, often writing at home—perhaps he was doing this long before I came to the school, without having an outlet for his work. I never got to know Jeff well, our meetings were always brief and hectic. The last time I saw him, he told me that he was working on a novel. . .

THE HORIZON

"The Horizon was as bright as a flashlight. This was the result of mankind."

Let's start from the beginning, or should I rather say, "the beginning of the end." It all started to 1969 when talk started about ecology. For the next 23 years the talk went in and out of people's ears, just like poverty and violence. But then one day the world got so loud it was impossible not to hear or see the disaster.

July 12, 1992 was the day. The day everyone woke up unable to see the sunlight. It was blacker than any night. But the people, still blinder than they ever were, used some other device as an answer. Electricity was found to be the most useful device in the process of the dark day.

Now it was time for all people to worry and wonder. Was it us who created the dark day, or is it a punishment. This was also the time to go through all history. But you and I know it only started 23 years ago. So they went through thousands of years. These were years of hardship. But they were still too blind to see that it was their fault.

Finally, the day ended. It ended in hope that tomorrow they could see the light of the sun.

It finally came, tomorrow was now today. But still with the Blackness of yesterday.

Today the scientists found a solution. The solution presented up with another problem. "War." They figured out this very unscientifically. They thought that Europe had made the darkness because of a few years ago. This was when we (the U.S.) started to think of a new food producing method. Europe at that time was a complete rural area of the country and the peace of hundreds of years ago. They must have decided to be rid of us. Their idea must have been to make a sheet of black over us. They knew that we couldn't survive without the sun for more than two weeks. For we were not that well advanced in science to produce an artificial sunlight. They also must have thought that this would close us in with our dirt and pollution.

It was time to act. So we blew an atom bomb and aimed it to Europe. But our course was indirect and we hit Russia. Russia was waiting for this moment. So they released a new weapon to us. This weapon would shake the U.S. apart until it was mutilated. So we started to shake and we started to die. We were doomed. So we were destroyed. We were now just history.

If we were only smarter. Smart enough to have done something in 1969. Smart enough to realize it was *us*. Now it was the end for all of us. That is, the world was doomed. For the chain reaction was too much for the world. We were about to fall apart anyway.

So now, 2001, there was light and the Horizon Was As Bright As A Flashlight. This was the result of mankind.

by Jeff Weiss

JEFF WEISS'S SECOND:

PART I: WHERE I BELONG

After going to a party I was walking home all alone. I was so scared that every time I heard a sound I started to run. Then it happened—just what I didn't want to happen. Somebody put his arm around my neck and said that he wanted my money. I told him I didn't have any money but he still insisted. He hit me a few times and stuck a knife in me and ran. I fell to the ground crying. I tried to scream but blood would rush out of my mouth. I even remember a cop-car passing by. I knew this was it (the end of me). I started thinking about the party and how I wished I didn't go!

Now it began. Everything was coming at me at once.

"I told you not to go out late."

"Jeff, you make me sick."

"I don't want to go."

These were a few memories. Now life was like a strobelight. The pain was so much that I started to black out. Then as if a second passed by I heard someone say,

"How do you feel?"

I opened my eyes and I saw a lady in a white suit. I was in the hospital.

Weeks passed and I finally went home. I wonder what my friends will think now.

The next day I went to school, but it was just like it was before. Then in class I started to day dream. I dream about a heaven that I would go to if I had died. A man in white showed me the way and before I knew it I had wings. I started to fly. I didn't want to stop. It was just so much fun. So he let me fly for the rest of the day. But I didn't know where I was going. I started going down, but was stopped by a man in red. Then that man in white came and they were pulling on me. One had my left hand and the other had the right hand.

Then I woke up it was a dream. Everything wasn't real, it was all a dream.

Then the man in white came and said, "Time to eat." *So I flew away with him!*

PART II: IMAGINARY, OR WAS IT?

The walls of my room were getting smaller. What could I do? I ran for the door and grabbed the handle but it disappeared. By now the room was so small it could only hold me, but the room still got smaller. Finally it got so small I couldn't move.

Then just as fast as it happened the walls were gone. Now I was in just space. But it was not dark. It was filled with brilliant colors. Then the colors got so bright I couldn't keep my eyes open.

Now I was sitting in a room with two people sitting near me.

One said, "What do you think of it?"

The other answered, "He probably doesn't speak."

"I do!" I exclaimed.

"Ahhh. . ., he speaks."

"What the hell is—"

"Now, now , watch your language," the thing said.

I don't know why, but my mind kept on saying they are things and they are different! But they were as normal as I was. Now I started to wonder whether or not I was normal. Now, just like everything else, they were gone.

"STOP!" I screamed.

And there I was back in my room. My mother walked in and said, "Time to go to bed." I didn't tell her what happened because I was sure she wouldn't believe me. (Would you?)

The next morning in class my teacher presented us with a new student. I thought I would die—because it was one of those, those. . . things in my journey. He looked at me and smiled!

PART III: IMAGINARY, OR IS IT?

Friday night my friend slept over. We talked, and I told him my Journey as a dream. He looked at me and said, "Is this a joke?"

"Why?" I questioned.

"Because I had a dream like that, but, but. . ."

"What?!" I shouted.

"It wasn't a dream!"

"I hope you believe this, but I didn't dream it either."

Then he started to fade away and I screamed,

"Come back! Oh, God, what do you want with me?"

The cycle repeated. Just like a carbon copy. I was confronted with them again. One of their faces had changed. It was the one of the boy in school.

It was like looking in the mirror. I kept on seeing the same thing over and over. I wanted to tell someone. I started to think I was crazy. So I spoke to a teacher. The teacher told me that I may really need help.

Now, when I think back, I can't remember who anyone was. My friend, the teacher, me!

"WHO AM I?"

After the cycle repeated that same boy from the beginning came back to me. He said,

"Now you are one of us."

"One of what?"

"US," whatever it was said.

"I don't care anymore. Just tell me why I have been going crazy."

"Let me tell you what this is about," it said. "You see, it is a test. A test to see if you can handle a 10th level brain."

"What?"

"When you were normal like everyone else, you used 1/10 of your brain, or 1 level."

"Oh! So I must have a superior brain, right!"

"Yes, but since you human beings are so emotional you cannot handle a 10th level brain. But now it is too late, late, late,

late,

late,
  late,
    la. . . ."

"Take it Away!" I don't want to be smart!"

"I heard it again: "too late, late, late, late, la. . . "

I fell to the floor. Hours must have gone by. I must have fallen asleep. Now I was surrounded by kids. They were acting crazy. Wherever I went, they were there. I tried to explain to them, but they were too dumb to understand. I couldn't communicate with anyone!

Then the room shrank as everyone disappeared. The cycle for the 3rd time repeated. But at the end of the journey, I was in a hall and my mother was holding my hand. She led me into a room with a sign that said

MENTAL WARD

She left me in the room. There was the boy. That same one.

He looked at me, and he smiled.

PART IV: "BRING IN MR. WEISS"

Two men in black suits with masks over their heads came into the room in which I was standing. The room was pure white. Nothing in it, and no doors or windows.

They each grabbed one of my arms and lifted me up and carried me out of the room. They brought me before a statue that was pure red and was carved to resemble their leader (the man that called for me).

One said, "Whatever you want to do to our leader, do it to him now."

So I spat on the statue. The two men probably got mad because they chained me up and kept on slapping my face.

Then the leader came in and commanded, "leave me alone with the prisoner."

They left, and the leader continued, "When was this peaceful man elected for president?"

I said, "in 1961." But I don't see why he asked me that.

"Did any of your relatives vote for him?"

"Yes," I answered nervously.

"Do you think that I'm good looking?"

"Yes," I said again.

"Is that all you can say?" he said, as he slapped me. He went out of the chamber, but I could still hear him whispering. I really didn't make out any of the words. I wondered what they were going to do to me. I also wondered if anyone was worried about me back home. No matter how bad I felt inside, I couldn't get myself to cry.

Then those men came back to get me. They carried me into another room and put me into a plastic tube about 6 feet high and 2 feet in diameter. Then one of them got behind a switchboard and pressed a couple of buttons.

A few lights flashed, but I didn't feel any change in myself. My face started to itch. It felt like little pricks on my face. Soon it went away.

They put me in a room. Everywhere there were mirrors. All I had to do was take one look at myself. When I finally did I almost fainted. I looked just like him, the leader.

Then they gave me this sort of brain wash that made me do certain things even though I didn't want to do them. I was then put in a different tube and one of those men pressed a button and I was in another place. I had a gun in my hand. I clenched my hand and shot the gun. I didn't mean to but I just did it.

I really don't know what happened then. Everything went black. I began getting dizzy. I even remember I threw up. Whenever I try to open my eyes I would see police—hundreds of them. One lifted me up. And when I finally opened my eyes again I was back at that priosn. I never was really sure what it was.

I was in that same mirror room. Now above it was a monitor which let me see where I just was. And I saw that leader being carried into a police car.

One of those men came in and said, "Now I'm free. You see, he brainwashed us into being his slave and made us brainwash you. Everything backfired 'cause he ended up taking your place. Now he's going to jail for good."

"Why," I asked.

"Because you killed the President!"

Jeff Weiss
I.S. 70 – Grade 8
Winter 1971

Schools

This was my last session with the whole sixth grade class. (Following it I worked with a smaller group from the class—usually seven or eight kids—in our own room.) In many ways the session was profoundly disappointing. The kids had asked me to write about an imaginary school, an opportunity I had welcomed because I thought it was potentially a very exciting and natural topic for the kids themselves. A few months before I had found an article in the *Harvard Educational Review* by Robert Coles called "Those Places They Call Schools." I found this article particularly moving because Coles had been able to encourage children to offer real and serious criticism of schools as well as concrete suggestions for their improvement. Coles had worked with a tape recorder, talking with the kids and frequently inviting them to express their ideas through drawing and painting. I had hoped that our writing about schools might move in a parallel direction, that is slightly away from the humorous and fantastic toward ideas more closely related to the daily lives of the children. In writing my imaginary school piece, then, I rejected parody and fantasy and tried to figure out as honestly and seriously as I could what a "perfect school day"—a day dedicated solely to learning, might be for me. The school that I described was one that welcomed everyone, form children to senior citizens; there were no teachers (we were all part-time teachers and students), and no two rooms that looked the same (some were for large meetings or performances, others for small group activities, still others for total privacy.)

The kids wanted to know right away if I had done my homework. So I began the class by reading the piece. They listened quietly, respectfully, and with real engagement. From the moment I read the first sentence I realized that what I had written for the class was totally inappropriate. Good teaching may depend to a large extent on knowing what is possible. I had failed to take proper note of what was probably the most essential fact in Coles' work, namely that he had known the kids he had interviewed for three or more years and that he had earned thier complete trust.

Fortunately the class was not a total loss for few of the children actually chose to write about schools. We repeated our large list of possible topics from the previous week and once again I spread out their earlier work on the shelf in the back of the room so that the children had many options. The few school pieces were total disasters ("homeroom is my favorite time in school," etc., etc.). I doubt that the kids Coles interviewed were any more alienated from school than to an adult (especially one whose relationship to the school is as mysterious as my own) does depend on a great deal of trust, and I have not been around long enough to achieve it, even assuming that I could.

EXCERPTS FROM ROBERT COLES' ARTICLE, "THOSE PLACES THEY CALL SCHOOLS":

. . . the children I am soon to quote. . . are so-called "elementary school children." They are black and white. They either live in the ghetto of a large northern city or they live in sections called "white lower-middle-class" by sociologists and (so I heard all during 1968) "backlash-prone." I have known them, the boys and the girls, for at least three years—some of them for four going on five. I have visited them again and again and I think we have together a good "relationship." That is, we get along. We dig each other. We laugh and get suspicious and talk about a lot of nothing and about a lot of something and about a lot of everything and about "a plenty lot," as Margie put it once. Now, in the autumn of 1968 I asked Margie "a plenty lot" about her school, about the building in contrast to the usual questions about the things going on inside the building—the teachers, the lessons taught or not taught, the way things are done and handled and organized and regulated and and allowed to occur.

Margie is concrete. She talks about "those places they call schools," I don't know if you need to have schools in buildings. Those places they call schools, they're really no good. You know why? It's because they're not schools, I mean they're a place where they force you to go, and you sit there, and the teacher, she's tired and all she wants is for the clock to go round and round until it's time to leave. Maybe if the teacher was different, then she could come and help us out right here. My mother says there are enough of us in this building here, so we could have a school—maybe in our kitchen, it could be. Then we could get a cookie sometime (no, they don't have them, and no hot lunches either, or anything like that) and we could be doing something, not just sitting there and each of us laughing at what a joke it is.

I'll tell you one thing, I'd tear *this* building down. There's nothing to do but that. Then, if I could build a new school, I'd make it pleasant-like. I'd get rid of all the desks, every one of them. I'd have us sit around a table, and maybe we could have cookies. I'd have the teacher be better. She could laugh a lot, and there wouldn't be a clock up there, making noise every minute that goes by. We could open and close the windows and they wouldn't be stuck like now. We could have a big rug here in the room, so if you fell down you wouldn't get hurt, like I did. And they could have some places, some big sofas maybe, where if you didn't feel too good, you could lie down, or you could just sit in them sometimes, and you'd be more comfortable.

I'm not sure why they have us go to school. Do you know? Is there anyone who does?

I know it's to learn things, how to read and do arithmetic and like that, but most of the time it's just a waste, and you'd think they might want to change it around, and have us spend the day better. You'd think they might try to change a lot of things themselves. The principal himself, he complains to us that the big hall, it's too big, and you can't hear good, and the corridors, they're just too long and you practically should have a car to travel from one part of the building to the next. My older brother, he's in the sixth grade, and it's like he's across the country from me. I never see him except when school is out. Then everyone wakes up.

[Margie's brother Arthur:]

Well, I'll tell you, the whole place, it's pretty bad. I'll tell you why, I will. My sister said it was like a jail the other day, but it's not a jail, because you can leave, and if your mother will let you, a lot of the time you can just stay home and they don't really care, anyway. But when you're in there, in that building, I guess it does get pretty bad, like Margie said. I step and fall, because the floors are no good; they're too smooth and you can hear everyone walking and it's like in a war, in a battle, the teacher said. The windows, no one ever looks in them or looks out of them. My friend Jim put his finger on one and there was so much dust he could write his name, and then the teacher got mad. What's the window for, though? We'd have to climb up on ladders to see through most of it. The bathroom, like Margie said, it's no good. They should have one for our home-room, one for each one, and then we wouldn't be walking all over, and it would be ours; and that goes for eating, too. I mean, why couldn't they have a kitchen for us like at home? My mother said if they can build these fancy apartment buildings so you can each have your refrigerator and your bathroom, they could do it for us in school, and then the whole place would be better, because we'd have a nice room

66

and you wouldn't have to go a mile and then find a big bathroom
and you can get lost in it and by the time you get back you've
missed everything they've been talking about. Then if they send
you out for the recess it's a joke. They tell you to watch out for
the glass and the cracks in the cement, but they never do anything to get rid of them.

I'd like comfortable chairs, like ones that had cushions so
your back doesn't hurt and your bottom either.

I'd like us sitting around—you know, looking at each other,
not in a line, not lined up. I'd like a sink, where you could get
some water to drink, and you wouldn't have to ask the teacher
to go down the hall, and half the time she says no. I'd like for
them to have cokes, not only milk, and they could have them
cold, and we could have our cups and there'd be a table and it
would be a lot nicer home-room than it is now. We could have
our books in a bookcase, and we wouldn't have to sit in the same
place all the time, and you feel it's like you're glued to the chair,
and the chair is glued to the floor (it is) and you can't move a-
round and if you do she'll shout at you to sit down and shut up
and mind your own business.

You know what? I'd like to be able to take off my shoes
and relax. The floor is so cold, you can't do that now. And they
could do better than having the room like it is—you can't put anything anyplace except where it's supposed to be, inside your desk.
She'll give you something to read, the teacher, and then she'll
have to take it away and put it in the cabinet and lock it up. If I
could do what I'd like, I'd have TV, and popcorn and you could
put our books on a table, spread them out there, and it would
make a nicer room.

In his home-room there might even be curtains and a magazine stand and lamps "like at home" and not only school books
but other kinds of books and "better pictures" on the wall, and a
tea kettle and of course a stove and some candy and a lot of
doors that opened up to the next rooms "on either side" and
plants and flowers and "most of all, really most of all" a window
in the roof so you could

> just look up and see the sky and the clouds and the sun
> and when the rain falls you could see it falling
> and you'd like it better, being in school.

Arthur himself, in a way, took the responsibility of discrediting his own
complaints:
Even if they built the best school building they could, it wouldn't
mean much if those teachers were the way they are, and if it kept
on being the way it is—a pain, I think. My uncle, he says you'll
have to change a lot more than buildings if you're going to make

it easier for us to get by. That's the way I think, too. Maybe I'm too hard on my teacher, and that school—the building, I mean—because like I say, the school, well it's not the real enemy, that's what my uncle says. He says we could take that school, bad as it is, if it wasn't that a lot of other things, they're even worse, even worse than it.

Miles away on tree-lined streets that no one would ascribe to a ghetto, live children as old as Margie and Arthur, but white and from homes that are called "single-family" and "middle-class." The fathers who own those homes are office workers, firemen and policemen (who frequently hold down two jobs and whose wives, often enough, work) and not the least, school teachers. The children go to a relatively new school, but still have their criticisms to make. Susan, for example, is Margie's age:

I'm pretty good at school. My mother says if I keep it up, I'll get to college, and it's not easy for a girl, not in our family, because there's just so much money, and it has to go for my brothers, if they can get in. If I could build a school, I guess play make-believe and do it that way, play magic, I'd make the school warm and small and not big and too hot one minute and you're shivering the next. I'd have a lot of little schools. I'd have every home-room a school, separate from the rest. Then there wouldn't be all those big buildings, and you get lost in them. My mother says I got scared, the first time I went to school, because it was so huge, and you couldn't see to the end of the hall; it just went on and on. And it's too dark in school; way too dark. And once you're inside, you never see the outside until the big bell rings and you can leave, if the teacher says yes, it's o.k.

A lot of the time, I think, if they put on the radio, like we have at home, it would be better than not hearing anything but yourself and the clock. The teacher, she always coughs and says it's time to do the next thing, and you can tell when she gets angry, because her chair squeaks a lot, because she moves around more. They should get rid of that chair. And they shouldn't have us to go to the bathroom way down the hall, and they told us that the lunchroom, it's too big and everyone gets lost in it. My mother says we could have little sun-rooms, with plants in them, and we could go and eat there, a few of us in each one, and it would be cozy. And I think we could have places to play, not just the halls and the classrooms and nothing else. Yes, we have the gym, but that's for games, and it's too big, and I mean a room like we have at home, a play-room, for our class; and other class-es, they could have theirs, too.

Billy, a couple of years older, lives across the street from Susan. He supported her view and added some other things too:

They should divide schools up, so you get to know the part you're in, as if it was your home or your friend's home. They should have a movie theatre there, and we could watch TV and it would-

Billy

n't be in the big auditorium, where it's too big and the seats are no good. They should have a fire-place or something like that in the room, so we could sit around it, and that would be better than those desks, especially if you're put in the back row like I am. They should have it more like home when you eat lunch, and not like it is, with the cafeteria and everyone trying to eat at once and a lot of the time you can't get a seat, and when you get one, it's no good anyway—those benches! And worst of all is the stairs—climbing them all the time, and you feel you'll get lost trying to find out which floor you're supposed to be on, and where the right room is. They could build buildings that are better: nicer and friendlier and the kind you can get to know every corner of it in a short while. I'll bet I could.

I took Billy and the other children up on that; I asked Billy to do exactly what he said he could do; and he did indeed sit down on several occasions and draw his school. As he drew and after he had drawn he talked. He told me how important it was that a school building be strong, and able to survive snow and rain and strong winds and the wear of thousands, of millions of footsteps. He told me that the buildings should beckon and welcome and reach out and say hello and a big goodbye and in general be something more, much more, than the word "building" implies. He put his feeling like this:

This school I'm doing, it will be liked by everyone in it. They'll say, isn't this a great place.

Billy and his friends build huts and hideouts and tents and cabins and forts— and do things to make those buildings livable, even lovable. They arrange and rearrange. They decorate and embellish and add and subtract: wood, leaves, rags, sticks, rocks, all the "materials" that architects and designers and engineers talk about. They struggle for privacy, yet they want to make themselves and their choices and preferences and works and constructs apparent, very

69

much so. They insist on the integrity of their own decisions and judgements, yet at the same time they constantly call upon the authority of their parents— and not necessarily out of begrudging obedience or fear.

A month later Billy, and his friend Gerry got together and Gerry, more of an "idea-man," as he calls himself (he got the term "on television") told Billy what to draw, because, in Gerry's words,

> I can't draw, not even a straight line with a pencil and a ruler to do it . . . A good school would have a road going right through it, or under it, and you could see cars and stores and people, and they'd be looking at you, and then you wouldn't have to take a bus and go way out into nowhere, just because you're going to school. . . . They shouldn't drag us all over the city, just to see some pictures in a museum and places like that. They could have a big room in the school, and we could go and look at things all the time, if we wanted, not just once a year. They could even hang our pictures, and the teacher, she should try drawing, the teacher should. She told us she wasn't any good at it, and neither am I; but some teachers are good painters, I'll bet, and they would probably like everyone else to see what they've done.

Billy

Margie draws her school reluctantly; she is bored and in time outspokenly annoyed:

There's nothing to draw, except those big walls. That's all school is, a big brick building, and all the stupid stuff inside. Half the time I'm ready to fall asleep, and half the time the teacher is just as sleepy. If you want me to make up a *good* school, then I could try. I think the best thing to do is tear down the old school and let it be a place for us to play, the land. Then we could build a-nother one, and it would be better. Outside it would have statues of our people, black leaders, like I saw in the news they had some-place, in front of some building. And you could walk right inside. They'd have a garden with rocks and water and flowers, just like they had in the museum and there'd be a bridge over the water, like they had in the museum and there'd be a bridge over the wa-ter, like there is there; and you could walk inside a room like in the other museum, and they'd have a map of the world on the walls, all around everywhere, and you could stand and see all the continents and the oceans.

Margie's brother, Arthur, has a hero, a youth named Jack, a tough more-than-youth: at fifteen he is a "child" —still required to attend school—who is also very much a grown man. Jack talks, talks a lot. Jack is in junior high, and at sixteen will certainly leave school. For Jack the ghetto has other schools, schools that offer something, maybe everything he has decided he wants. He stays on not because school officials pursue him and compel him to stay, but because his father, his step-father in fact, insists it is necessary and desirable:

Margie

The old man, he's up against the ropes. He's broke. He used to have some money, but they cut him off, the people he worked for. Now, he's got nothing, and he thinks I'll get nothing, too, un-less I go to school—which is crazy. His brother, he finished high school, and he never could find a good job. They say now you can, because they want the black man for display, and they're scared, too. But man, we're too many, and they only want a few.

These schools, they're real old, like all the other buildings here, and even when they build a new one, they know it'll become just like everything else in a day or two it will—because it can't help being like that. The rat that bit my kid sister, he's not going to stop and say "Well, well, what a nice school, I think I'll stay

71

clear of it." And anyway, they'll always be those teachers, driving up in their cars and looking both ways when they get out and locking them. They forget that a man like my step-father, he can't afford the gas, even if he drove off with the car. But I'll have a car and there'll always be gas in it, I can bet you on that.

As far as school buildings go, they're all no good, any I've seen. I told Arthur they should forget the whole thing. Let some of those teachers come over here and talk with us—I mean, in our homes, or at the pool hall. As soon as they get together under one roof, even if it's all glass, like Arthur says it should be, then you're sunk. It's no good. All they want is for us to be quiet and polite and mind them. They are glad when school is out and they can get away from here. And what they teach you, it's enough to make you drowzy, drowzy all day.

Arthur says if they changed the way schools are, then he'd stay. But how can they? They'll never do it. You think they'll tear down that school of Arthur's and build one like he drew over there? That's a joke.

Arthur

At the opposite extreme, children at the MUSE* writing workshop in Brooklyn who worked with poet David Shapiro created one of the most extraordinary school fantasies I have ever seen. Lacking the trust which might have encouraged more realistic writing, this should have been my starting point. In fact, a few weeks later, I gave "Learn Something, America" to the kids to read, and they were delighted with it.

---

*Brooklyn Children's Museum which sponsors a number of workshops in the arts for children.

LEARN SOMETHING, AMERICA

My school is made out of bricks and it looks wonderful on the outside, but when you step inside, it's terrible. I go up the stairs; it's muddy. Everybody spills milk on the stairs, papers, lost notebooks, bookbags, pencils, that that when you step on them they take you down the stairs, in other words break your neck. Everybody's racing up the stairs and the line is going down. I fall down the stairs and my clothes get dirty. Everybody starts laughing: "There he goes again."

Everybody's half asleep in my class when I get inside. The classroom is worse than the rest of the school: papers on the floor, notebooks all over the desk, books thrown all over the floor. Miss Grunchy, who eats your head, is in the back of the class. The line that's supposed to be a straight lovely line, is scattered all over the room. Miss Grunchy hollers, "Keep quiet and sit down. Get off the floor." Nevada says: "Shut up," under his breath of course. Gina, who never lets Miss Grunchy hear her talking says: "Shut your big mouth before I sock you right in the nose. We aren't even settled yet and she starts with all her misery, making the rest of the class unhappy, as if we weren't already."

I call a boy in my class French Potato because he keeps on getting me in trouble, because he's French. And every time he makes some kind of noise he says I'm doing it. Then he says: "You wanna fight me?" Then when we get outside he runs across the street; he runs home. Class is finally settled and the first thing we do is the Pledge of Allegiance. Everybody starts blowing his nose. Miss Grunchy says: "Say the Pledge of Allegiance, class." We begin:

I pledge to a fathead Miss Grunchy
I don't pledge allegiance to the flag
because Miss Grunchy makes me mad
when Miss Grunchy eats her lunch
     she slops
it all around and she eats it off
the floor and she eats nails; she eats
nails, iron, mice, cardboard,
grasshoppers, paper, fish, and
     students.
She doesn't have to tell us what she
     eats—
from the papers she marks you can
tell what she's had for dinner or
for breakfast, she's so sloppy.

One class under Miss Grunchy in
     misery
With unjustice for the whole class.

So we killed Miss Grunchy. She turned back to life and she got meaner. She teaches First grade mathematics to a sixth grade class. 1+1=2 — because she doesn't know it herself, she has to ask us what it is. So the principal kicks her out of school, and didn't we have a better teacher? The new teacher's name was Mrs. Sweetypie.

Mrs. Sweetypie gives us sugar every day; it tastes terrible. When we go home we go to the dentist. Mrs. Sweetypie teaches us tenth grade arithmetic and in the middle of it she gives us candy to get our minds back to the same old class next term; we get left back again; only one of us passes. What kind of a Sweety Pie is she?

When we go into the lunchroom we have to form a line. The cook's name is Mrs. Sloppy Joe Pancake Mix and her helper is Mrs. Messy Fingers. They stick their fingers into our food and we throw it on their heads. They don't wash their hands, so we go buy pizza for lunch. When we're there they're the same cooks. Same people cooking at the same place. We feel as if we have to get out of the city to get a decent lunch. So our mothers take us SOUTH.

Meanwhile back in the lunchroom the poor children put their pork and beans in the milk.

In the auditorium we have assembly every Friday. Every Friday night there's singing and dancing. We pledge allegiance again. There's nothing in the Winky Eye program but eyes; all different colors—rainbow colors, black, yellow, green, bronze, yellow. The children get bored so they start talking. The girls talk about boyfriends; the boys talk about roaches. The girls talk about what they'll be when they grow up; the boys talk about lizards, rats, dirt from the sewer. The girls would like to be nurses; the boys would like to be superheroes.

The science program is about Our Eyes. They tell you all the stuff you know, like your eyes make you see; you have pupils in your eyes; you have lenses in your eyes; you have all different kinds of parts in your eyes, and that you have to dissect a cow's eye so you can see all the different colors in it that help us to see the colors that are around us. The teacher says: "Hush your mouth and eat your candy. You have lots more." We eat the candy as long as they don't find out. She calls us African animals. She says we eat our candy like we're a whole bunch of monkeys, gorillas, elephants, mosquitoes, ants, rats and lizards.

They think they're so wonderful, especially last year's teacher, Mrs. Broccoli. She always used to walk around the classroom with her head stuck up in the air walking like she was so wonderful. She'd tell us not to talk and in the middle of class the next door neighbor Mrs. Noteeth walks in the class. She can't stand one minute without batting her eyelashes and she talks: "Marcia did you hear about blablablablablablablablabla b-b-b-b-b-b- lalalalala-la John and Susan and Elizabeth are going to the Palisades Park," and she keeps talking on and on while batting her eyelashes. When we fail our math lessons, then she says we were talking when we were supposed to be doing our work!

Then she says we should have a suggestion box. So we made some suggestions:

1) DON'T HAVE THE TEACHERS SO MEAN AND STRICT
2) DON'T HAVE ANY TEACHERS AT ALL
3) DON'T HAVE TEACHERS SO PREJUDICED AND HAVE THEM SPEND SOME MORE TIME TEACHING US INSTEAD OF TALKING ABOUT THEIR SOCIAL AFFAIRS
4) KICK ALL TEACHERS OUT OF SCHOOL
5) YOU SHOULD HAVE A CHILD FOR PRINCIPAL OR ASSISTANT PRINCIPAL SO HE COULD HAVE HIS VIEWS ON HOW THE SCHOOL SHOULD BE RUN AND ALL THE CHILDREN BEAT HIM UP AND HE STARTS CRYING AND THEN HIS MOTHER'LL COME UP AND HE'LL SAY, "I'M GONNA SUSPEND YOUR MISERABLE CHILD," SO HE SAYS: "I QUIT."
6) I SUGGEST EAT RAT SOUP, SPIDER SOUP, CAMBELLS SPIDER-MILK SOUP
7) I SUGGEST WE DRINK CHOCK FULL OF NUTS AND BOLTS
8) AND EAT HOSTAGE FRUIT PIES
9) TEACHERS AND STUDENTS SHOULD HAVE MORE SOCIAL RELATIONSHIP, GET TO KNOW EACH OTHER SO YOU CAN UNDERSTAND EACH OTHER'S PROBLEMS. NOBODY UNDERSTANDS US POOR UNDERESTIMATED KIDS
10) LEARN SOMETHING, AMERICA.

THE END

by some members
of the class

The SUTEC Workshop

After several months' work at I.S. 70 I began to feel that the Utopias theme was very promising and that it would be helpful to expand into other classrooms. I was excited enough at this point to want to collaborate with other teachers on the project. One of our writers had been working at P.S. 76 in Long Island City, Queens, and he recommended the school as an extremely welcome place to work.

This is exactly what it turned out to be. P.S. 76 is an experimental public school, the experimental aspect under the auspices of the School University Teachers Education Center program of the Queens College Department of Education. SUTEC provides in-house training for pre-service teachers by placing them in classrooms with experienced teachers who are themselves graduates of the Department. The program saturates a school with its own people (teachers and trainees) for maximum effect. The direction of the training is toward more open classrooms, and there is an atmosphere in which real innovation and experimentation is possible. The program is directed by Dr. Lucille Perryman whose personal energy has much to do with the program's success.

Initially I met with about a dozen teachers and trainees in the SUTEC Program. Of these, four (all regular teachers) were interested in setting up a new writing workshop on Utopias. The four teachers were Selma Bokor, Barry Rader (both sixth grade teachers), Violet Ellis (fourth grade), and Eleanor Kaplan (third grade). The workshop became a new and exciting experience for us since we were able to break down the traditional "expert/teacher-in-training" roles which had plagued many of our workshops with teachers in the past. In the beginning, of course, I discussed my experience in working with Utopias and, throughout, I had more time than the teachers for collecting additional source materials. Otherwise, within a few weeks, we were on an equal footing, searching for new approaches to teaching the theme, sharing our failures along with our successes, and comparing the student work which emerged from our classes. Finally, what became truly exciting about the workshop, was that each teacher found ways to integrate the Utopias project into his regular program, in a manner that was compatible with his own teaching style. We met regularly, once a week, during lunch hours. There was never enough time to discuss all the material that was brought to the sessions.

Barry Rader invented a whole series of marvelous letter-writing assignments. "You are carried away by a stranger to a mysterious place, you are allowed to write home to your parents, telling what has happened to you." "You live for two weeks in an imaginary land, you write another letter home, telling them what the place looks like." Of all of us, Barry was able to develop the most cohesive writing in response to the theme. He had worked extensively with writing in his own classroom in the past (often devoting an hour a day to it) and had developed lists of hundreds of writing ideas which he had used in his classroom. (See May-October 1971 Teachers and Writers Collaborative Newsletter for his own statement about his work in writing.) His class continued the letter writing idea for seven or eight weeks. Then they edited and revised the letters, added illustrations, and made a whole set of class utopian novels. I happened to visit the class just when the books were being completed, and could not help noticing the obvious pride which his kids took in their accomplishments.

Eleanor Kaplan integrated the imaginary worlds idea with a study of weather which was already underway in her classroom. The class produced some wonderful work on imaginary weather. Later, her class also began work on a number of class books, written and illustrated by the children. I regret that we do not have the children's work from her class to reproduce here to reflect her contributions.

Selma Bokor's class was freewheeling and open. She would write a suggestion for creative writing on the board in the midst of twenty other activities. Almost imperceptibly, the other activities would be swept away and her kids began writing. She seldom addressed the whole class; if children had questions about the idea, or wanted to ask her whether they could work on something else instead, they met with her individually. We disagreed on the value of reading as a crutch; I was determined to continue to bring such works to the kids. We had many interesting talks about this, and the issue was never resolved. But it was obvious that my approach to writing would have been hopelessly out of place in her classroom.

Mrs. Violet Ellis works with her children on a very individualized basis. There is a heartwarming personal quality in her children's writing which indicates a close one-to-one relationship. The story "The Amazing Looking Stay-In Glass" was worked on for several days in her classroom; it is included in this section, along with a second touching fantasy. Mrs. Ellis's children have been represented before in Collaborative Newsletters. (See "Metaphors," by by Art Berger, in the January 1971 issue of the Newsletter—V.3, I.4.)

The section that follows contains some of the children's work from P.S. 76 that grew out of our shared interest in children's writing in general, and Utopias in particular. We wish we could have produced a larger publication to more justly reflect the contributions of the SUTEC workshop, which were vital to the development of the whole Utopias project.

FROM MRS. ELLIS' CLASS

THE AMAZING LOOKING STAY-IN GLASS

Once upon a time there lived a girl by the name of Mary Wile. Now one day she was passing an antique shop. Now Mary was with her mother and they two were going to an antique shop. Now Mary's mother's feet were very weary so she and her mother could not pass another antique shop so they stop at the antique shop they had just seen. Now Mary's mother was looking for a huge mirror like the one I just drawed for you. Well, anyway the man looked for a big tall straight carved shining looking glass. The man finally found the perfect looking glass that you could look at yourself in from head to foot and wow was that big. So Mary's mother asked how much it cost and the salesman said: $25.99 and the face on Mary's mother was a stunned face and more stunned was she until a couple of seconds passed by and she soon realize that she couldn't go to another store for her feet was murdering her, and it was late and Mary was hungry. So she said to the salesman: okay, you got me. And so she handed him the money and by the next day the mirror was safely delivered to Mary's mother. Now many days later passed quickly by. And Mary hadn't went out to play for the last 8 days, ever since the Mirror entered the house. Now many of her friends started to wonder odd and foolish things; one thought "is she being punish," another one thought, "Did she did something," another one thought, "Did she speak back to her mother badly," and one more thought "I wonder if her mother beat her" and now they were thinking more sillier and foolisher. But all the time they were thinking, she was only looking at herself in the big and huge mirror. One day while she was looking in the glass all alone not noticing nothing, all at once her dog barked and all at once again she jumped into the mirror into the LAND OF MIRROR and all she saw was big mirrors, small mirrors, medium mirrors, and huge mirrors. Every mirror she look in there was a dimension in each mirror, and one of those billion mirrors there was a mirror which would lead her back home. And just as she was looking at the thousands of mirrors a strange tall odd man step out of the mirrors and said to Mary, "Mary you and your mother was very Unwise to go into that shop and buy that horrible huge straight perfect mirror, for did you notice the name of the Shop?" asked the strange tall man. No, said Mary. I don't seem to remember. First she paused trying so hard to remember; and all at once she remember it and yell it to the man: Why yes, it was called the Future taking mirrors. Oh, no, said Mary, I didn't think that meant that. Oh yes, it did, said the weird man. That place no one goes to buy mirrors there. See that place was condemned many years ago. And people in the neighborhood said that it should be put on fire, cause the place was owned by an insane woman and the village said that they heard her whispering strange things and that made her neighbors say that she was a witch from evil. So a man in the village thought that this was most ridiculous and most of all nonsense, so he bought the place for a mirror, said the tall strange looking man. So that's why people were staring at me and my mother, and that's why the place was filled with nothing but mirrors, and nothing was hardly sold, said Mary. And the strange man nodded agreeably. And so here you are, said the man. Now I need to get out, said Mary to the strange man. Oh no, said Mary, I must have been here hours, said Mary. No, said the strange man, every hour you stay here it is a second in your house. Woo, said Mary in good relief. But how did you get here? said Mary to the strange looking man. The same way you got here. Anyway, help me get out of this horrible place, said Mary. Oh, said the man, now that's going to take a lot of time. Oh, I don't care, said Mary, ask me anything. All right, what time is it on earth? May 12, 1956. What time was it when you got here? About 1:05 turning to six. All right, come with me, said the strange man. He had led her into a mirror. He said jump in. Just about as she was going in she stop and said to the man, "Why aren't you going?" No, Mary, I belong here. No, you go. Just about as she was going in her eyes were fill, her small eyes, and ran to the man and had hugged him with a kiss and ran into the mirror, back to her time. And her mother said, where were you? Oh, just lookin in the mirror.

THE END

Joanna Caldas

MY DREAM

I went to the country. There was a nice dressmaker. I told her to make me a gown. I asked her to put pearls and flowers on my gown. We went to the church in a black car. In the car was me and my groom, bridemaids, flower girl, in the car to go to the church. And when we went to the church the people said that the gown was so beautiful and the bridemaids had a red dress. The flower girl had a blue dress and white shoes. There was many flower of all kind. There was roses, daffodils, carnations and many more. One day I found a dress—there was roses sewed on it and a gold line on my dress. It was from uncle—when I was 19. So I put it on and after a century it still fitted me and I put it on to the ball and we dance to 12 o'clock and we had fun, fun and we went home and went to bed. In the morning we was called to lunch, and we had wine, meat, potatoes, and we had a dance to the music all afternoon. We went for a walk in the moonlight in the garden, we went back to the dance and we went home. In the morning we went horse riding all morning, afternoon and night. We went back to the barn to put the horses in the barn and went home. The next day we went to a party—drink so much so we went for a ride.

It was Sunday and we was swimming all day and we had drink. It was a very hot day and we had cold cold drink and we was talking about some more clothes and some suit for my husband and I ask the bridemaids and the flower girl if they're wanting to stay at the house all weekend and go horse riding and dancing, swimming, going to party. It was springtime, the birds were sing and the squirrel was playing in the forest, the children was playing ing the forest, the children was playing in the park. I had ten children. Their names was John, Anthony, Michel, Glenn, Darrell, Laurie, Lisa, Linday Lynn, Lie. The first boy age is 6, the second boy's age is 7, the third boy age is 8, the fourth boy age is 9, the fifth boy age is 10. The first girl age is 11, second 12, third 13, the fourth is 14, the fifth 15 year old. And that is all my family and my husband. The week, week, week went by and the summer came and the people went swimming all day. We had fun and they had drink with others friends and weeks went by and it was fall, when Lie got maried to a man and they got married in the country under a tree where the leaves was falling on the ground and the 3 sisters was the bridemaids and one sister was the flower girl, and we had so much fun. For their honeymoon they went to the Skiing Lodge for 4 months, she got a lot of gift, and they wrote the children and me and my husband that they was having fun going skiing.

Linda

FROM MRS. BOKOR'S CLASS

My imaginary place look big and a stage that is real big. The people are males. They dress like other humans. They are not children—they're men. The Temptations sang alot. In this imaginary world, we live in a big house and I Go with my brother to practise.

I was going for a walk in the forest and I saw a rabbit. The rabbit said "I am not a rabbit, I am a boy." "OK, you are a boy." "I have a family—come to my house." "OK," said Barbara. The mother was a rabbit too. The boys was a rabbit too, and the girl was a rabbit too—all rabbits in the house. It was time for bed. The boys and girls went to bed. "Do you want to sleep here?" "Yes," said Barbara, "I will sleep here." The girls play ball, Barbara play ball too. I was playing ball and I saw Joann's mother and her mother put her to bed and I said, "I will go now."

The End

by Barbara T.

HOW TO GET TO MY IMAGINARY WORLD. . .

One day I was sitting down and I imagined I was in a boat and it was big and red. My family was with me until we got to a certain point. We met another boat—it was big and pretty. Everyone but me was getting on it. I was the only one that came in the red boat—funny—and when I was going to get out I turned red, but I kept on getting out, and someone said, "Ain't no sense in you getting out because you belong in the devil's care. . . ." and I said, "I was there for two years, and if you let me bring my family, I'll stay for two more. It's fun down there."

In my imaginary world the people are nice to me because when a bunch of bad people get together they all sense to be nice. They are all worn out and they look very bad. The clothes they wear is the clothes they had on when they die. There are all kinds of people. There is so many children there it's a shame.

Where my world is the outside is red and the inside is burning with fire, but the poeple don't burn until your time comes. The kind of family that are there is bad. You see the families are bad until they get to this world, then they turn good. Down there they don't have to work—they just wait to get burned and they also don't have any wars.

by Carrie Wright

To illustrate Barry Rader's "Letters From An Imaginary Land" assignment we are including one entire opus (Biagio Lodovici's *The Land of Destination*). In addition, there are several excerpts from the "Letters" of other children in his class.

THE LAND OF DESTINATION

Dear Folks

How do you feel. I am not the same any more because I changed when I got here. Now I am all fat and everyone looks very bad. And the man that came to our house, he was my teacher with a mask on. Now the boss of this land tied him from a tall tree and the small kids are hitting him on his belly. He is crying hard, and do you know why they put him up there? Because he wanted to run away with the big boss's wife, and he got caught and in 2 days they are going to execute him. The executioner was Dottry the top egg and if he kills Rader I will not be able to come back home and I will be stuck out here for the rest of my life. I will never see you again and I might die here in this bad place. I have a plan. I will try to make friends with the top egg and then I would put him to sleep and I try to cut off his head. But I don't think it will work because the yolk is rotten and the ax will break. I guess I am stuck here forever. But I have one more plan and maybe it will work. I will try to free Rader and tell him to get me back to my home land but I do not think he can do it any more because he forgot how to do it. I guess he is going out of his mind when the kids hit him in the stomach. If they keep on hitting him he will die so what will I do? Because I am scared here all by myself and if I get back I will never beg you to go some place. I will just stay home and dream about it. But maybe you can get me back. You can send a plane over and you can let me on and we can tie a rope around Rader's stomach and drag him along. But you would not know where to go with the plane so good bye its been nice seeing you. Your son. I will miss you.

Dear folks

When we left from our house the man put me in a bag. It was a very small bag, but he put me in there and I stayed in there for five whole hours. Then he put me out of the bag and he was beginning to change. I got kind of fat and I did not like it at all. I said "take me back" but he said that we could

THIS IS HOW THE PEOPLE LOOK

THIS IS THE BAG HE PUT ME IN AND HOW THE PLACE LOOKED WHEN HE TOOK ME OUT

never go back again. He put me in another bag and it was smaller and I got real mad and I said if we ever got back I would sue him but it was no use. He could not hear me while I was in the bag. I was feeling ugly. I tried to get out but I could not do it and the bag began to spin and I got real dizzy. The bag kept on spinning and spinning. I thought it would never stop but it did. When the man took me out I was almost dead. Then when I saw him he was worse than me. He was fat like a cow and he made me sicker than I was. Then he put me in a tiny bag and then the bag was turned upside down and all of the blood ran to my head and I thought I was going to turn green. Then he turned it back again and I felt sick and I stayed in the bag for two days. When he took me out I was fatter than ever but I could not believe it there was a whole bunch of people there and they were all fat and that is how I got there.

Dear folks

It was about 12:00 noon when the paper came and when I read the newspaper I saw what it said. There was going to be a war. And all of the sudden I heard the bullets flying around. But they were not real bullets. They were just pieces of rotten cheese. And if one of the pieces hit Rader he might eat it and get very fatter than he was now. So I got very mad and I ran to the top of a hill and told him to cut him down because if he didn't do he might get fat as a big cow. He took a knife and went to cut him down but a piece of cheese hit him in the head and his head fell off. A whole bunch of roaches and ants and marbles came out of that head. So I had to cut the rope myself. I did it but Mr. Rader could not walk because he got too fat. I had to drag him so I got him up to the top of a big hill and I saw that the army was just after me and Rader who made me sick by looking at him. So then I got an idea and I rolled him down the hill and he alone killed 13 of those men by rolling over them and then we found a place to hide so they could not find us and we are still here. Now we need some food, I mean I need some food badly. Well, I hope that you are all fine and I hope you don't have a war.

Dear folks

Well it is six weeks that I am here and we had a party yesterday. It was because they hanged Rader by the feet and they shaved off his beard. Then the funny part came. Every one was talking when the tree broke and Rader fell on the top egg because he was guarding him. Then Mr. Rader got away and he ran into the bushes. But he did not know that the bush was poison ivy but he still kept on running and then the top egg ran after him with egg noodles. He was going pretty fast and Mr. Rader was going slow because he was too fat. Then the top egg got him and took him back to town and every one was mad at him so they put him into the wine cellar for 2 days. When they took him out he was drunk as a pig and he was brainwashed and every-

THIS IS WHAT THE BABIES DO WHEN THEY WANT SOMETHING

thing they told him to do he did it. Then after four days he recovered and he had a hangover. When he was feeling better they put him on a board and then they called the top egg and one opened his head and took rotten eggs out and then threw them at Rader. When they finished they took him off of the board and they let him walk around for a while and he was stinking more than a dead dog. That is all I can say so do not worry about me too much because I am beginning to make friends here so good bye and I hope to see you soon.

Dear folks

I know it has been seven weeks but I have one more thing to tell you. Well Mr. Rader finally made friends with the men here and I am kind of happy. But I noticed one thing when the babies are born, there is no doctor. The husband does all of the work. The baby teaches himself and he learns. how to walk by himself and how to talk because they don't want him to be spoiled. They made him do everything alone and he learns better that way. But this is the sad part about it. Most of the babies don't make it and die but the parents didn't even care when they just throw them in the dump. Now they are getting ways of making pollution and they like it to breathe and they like the way it makes the streets nice and ugly. When I go out I see two small kids fighting over nothing and I go over and try to stop the fight and the bigger boys come and drag me away. They let the other boys fight until one of them gets killed and all of the people walk away from the dead boy. So I go and bury him and this is all I have to say. Your son.

THIS IS OUR PLANE.

Dear folks

This is just a letter to remind you that I will be coming home next week and I will tell you how I will get home. Well a couple of days ago I heard the big boss talking in private and he said that all of the people were eating too much and they would run out of food pretty soon. He said that if they did not find any food in two or three days they would have to start eating each other and Mr. Rader was all for the idea but then I found a book that the big boss dropped and it was a book to show me how to make an airplane and he said if I got him a bottle of whiskey he would help me. So I got him his whiskey and he said OK. So we began to make the plane and then the big boss found out that his book was gone so he searched all of the mud houses but he did not look in our house. I guess he thought we could not read. Well when we finished our plan we needed some gas and that was hard to get. So I tried to sneak some of it in to my mud house, but it was not long before the big boss found out his gas was gone, so I was very scared and I hoped that he would not look in our house and he didn't. So now I just need some more gas and the plane can leave with me and Rader on it. SEE YOU SOON

by Biagio Lodovici

87

MY IMAGINARY LAND

The people that lived there were very nice. They would say, "Please come in" if they didn't know you and they would say, "we won't harm you." And they would say, "I would just like to meet you." When Christmas came you would get presents from everybody because everybody would know you and even if they didn't know you so well, they would still say "HELLO" how are you doing.

by Theresa Bostic

MY IMAGINARY LAND AND ME

Dear Folks,

I am doing fine but I must tell you about the attack we had yesterday. It was just awful. We saw the armored elephants running down the land. They ran down all the orchards and flowers. They started to get the people. Everybody was terrified. They put me in the strange looking room with Harold my friend. We tried to think of some way to help them. My friend Harold thought of something. There is only one spot that the armored elephants are not covered and that is their stomachs. Another one of their weaknesses is to tickle their feet. We called for the king of wishes and we wished that the armored elephants would lie down on their backs and stay like that. He granted the wish and then everybody started jumping on their stomachs and tickling their feet. I asked the king of wishes to make them get up and go to the nearby cliff. They went on the cliff and all of them fell off the cliff right on their stomachs and died. We all had a big party and everybody was happy. That is all I have to say to you now.

Your son,
Miguel

MY DREAM COME TRUE

. . . .Oh mom and dad I do want to stay can we—Yes   or no   Tell all of my friends I said that I have miss them. That night the visitor came to my house to take me to the Imaginary land we had to go at night. I don't know why but when I got there I did. When we were at the front of the door then the visitor made sure that no one saw us and then up from the sky came down a rainbow. The visitor said step on the rainbow and the next thing we were going up, up, up, and then he said you will love the place you are going to—it is wonderful. On our way we passed by a lot of planets. We passed by Jupiter, Venus, Mars and Mercury. We almost got in a lot of trouble. People from Mars they tried to attack us but we got away. And then we came to a place where there was a lot of candy canes and he said so we are here now. . . .

by Debra

THE ADVENTURES OF CANDYLAND

Dear Folks,

Mrs. Willy Wonka came on time—3:00. I was all packed. There I was. No one was driving. But the car was there. So a little woman stepped out with a cane. She limped over toward me. I had a very big lump in my throat. I could not speak a word. I opened my mouth and no words came out. Then Miss Willy Wonka said "I am lonely now and need someone to talk to." I didn't ask anything when we went into the limousine. She said "Dear you mustn't be afraid of me or any of my servants. They're called Opooms." So I said that "you are very gentle and kind and I will not be afraid of you or your servant." We were on our way. I just layed back and watched the things go by. I still remember my parents and sisters and cousin and aunts and uncle. I cried. My heart sank as I left my family behind me. Miss Willy Wonka said stop. Then she took out a wand and wave it in the air. There was a ice cream cone in her hand. I wanted to say thank you but nothing came out. Then she said stop the car and it stop. We got out. Now it's time to go. I'll write again. Good Bye Now.

Love,
Denise

Henry Sneed

This diary summarizes the four or five sessions we spent working on the play.

I doubt that I would have ever started a play had it not been for Dick Gallup's work at P.S. 20. Dick had just recently completed a play with his fifth and sixth graders there, and his diaries, summarizing his work, seemed to me a very realistic description of what must happen when writing a play with a group of kids. In particular, he stressed that playwriting can be a long, slow process: "I must be sure that everyone understands each bit of action or dialogue before going on to something else. Also, there is the problem of getting them to agree that such and such is a good idea. It is also necessary to recapitulate just what happened, which characters are present, who is doing what, sitting where, etc. There is a tendency of the kids to give about three scenes worth of action in one idea and it is difficult to convince them to think only in terms of what *actually* happens next."

So, I was prepared for a long haul.

There was another compelling reason for wanting to begin a play. In my opinion some of the kids, through their prose writing, had already created characters with fantastic dramatic potential. One of these was Henry Sneed—perhaps the only character in Utopian literature to discover a new land because he was fed up with his wife (a real nag) and his kids (spoiled brats). Jason Brill added new adventures during my subsequent visits. But I felt Jason would soon tire of his character, unless given the opportunity to write about him in some new way. Here is one of the early Sneed sagas:

HENRY SNEED TRAVELS TO BLORKABOB

It was just an ordinary weekend for Henry Sneed, well it wasn't too ordinary because he went to a deserted fishing pond (you see he usually stays home) to read in quiet. His wife was a real nag and his kids were spoiled brats.

When Henry got to the fishing pond he decided to walk around it. He had started around when just a second ago where he saw just plain water was a clump of bushes now. He started over to it. He found there was something under it—it was something he'd never seen nor heard of in his entire life. It was long with things sticking out of it.

There was something that looked like a seat in the middle inside a cabin. He got inside and in front of the chair there was a control panel and just over the panel was a thing that said thingamabob # 108. He said to himself "thingamabob? that's a very funny name. I wonder what it does," and prompty pressed a button. Everything started to wrrrrrr. Everything was one big blur. He was going so fast he couldn't see where he landed. But he had landed. Slowly he climbed out of the "Thingamabob" and slowly looked around. He saw many strange plants and trees and the water was pink with purple polkadots. Then he saw these beings which were very pretty because they were all different colors. They said that they would like him to stay because they had seen him on America (this place was called ArkleBink) and we saw your wife and children nagging at you so we sent our thingamabob. Henry thought about it and consented and to this very day he's been living in ArkleBink happily ever after, or so we think.

Jason Brill

Next, there was Randy Besman's "Land of the Slobs and Neatlings," which he had invented in response to the imaginary war assignment. Here, potentially at least, was a cast of thousands (Slobs and Neatlings) already engaged in the most elemental of human conflicts. Originally I approached Jason and Randy to ask if they would like working on a play which would combine some of their ideas: a play in which Henry Sneed might visit the Land of the Slobs and Neatlings. They were delighted--possibly for the wrong reasons—I think the word "play" conjures up visions of finished performances in the school auditorium. So I had to be careful to point out that our play would probably never be performed, though we could certainly arrange to read it to the whole class. No matter, they told me, and soon we had rounded up three other kids—Marianne Ettisch, Peter Ortiz, and Howard Taikoff.

We begin with character descriptions, starting with Henry Sneed. I asked leading questions—what does he look like? what's he do?—and then wrote down the answers. By listing and defining our characters, I found that we were simultaneously developing the plot for the entire play. For example, after we had described Henry and his wife Bertha, I would say, "Ok, now who does Henry meet in the Land of the Slobs and Neatlings?" "A ruler, the king." "And what's he like?" etc. Then we decided that the play should have two love stories (Henry falls in love with a Neatling maiden, then a Slob maiden) and we talked about each of the female characters. The character descriptions themselves weren't too interesting, and are hardly worth reproducing. What was important was that we knew we had the groundwork for a complete play by the end of the session.

Nearly all the successful plays I have seen emerge from classrooms were developed as collaborations—a group of kids, sometimes a whole class, talking about the play, interpreting and speaking for the various characters, while the writer/teacher takes down the action and the dialogue. Originally, I saw no reason to depart from this procedure. But after two sessions, in which we completed only one short scene, I became quite dissatisfied with it. Dick Gallup was right in warning that it is a time-consuming process, that if you relax in your effort to keep the kids focused on the immediate action the whole play will come tumbling out. But these things did not bother me as much as the fact that the dictation method places an extraordinary amount of control in the hands of the teacher. I was simply unable to keep up with five kids, who often spoke simultaneously. The result was that I felt like a sort of filter whose primary function was to thin down the kids' natural styles. No matter how much I wanted to capture all that the kids were saying, there was no choice except to pick some lines, while the rest disappeared in the air. Nor were they necessarily the best lines, simply the ones that stuck in my mind long enough to write them. Certainly, a tape recorder might solve this, but there was another problem I found equally disturbing. Some of the kids are louder than others, become dominant, with the result that the characters they want most to interpret also become dominant. During one of our play-writing sessions, when Jason was absent, Randy decided to take charge of the character of Henry Sneed. So domineering was he in the role that Henry's character became quite distorted. This was the scene in which Henry leaves his wife, because she is a real nag. But it was Henry who emerged as the bastard, while poor Marianne Ettisch, who was trying to play Bertha, could barely get a word in edgewise. I stopped the action two or three times and went back to the character descriptions (so did some of the other kids, by the way; they, too, were quite aware of inconsistencies of character), but there was no stopping Randy.

The play is disappointing. It is *my* play, and lacks the style that these kids bring naturally to their own writing. I decided to risk a new approach. On 3 x 5 cards I typed a brief summary of each of the scenes we had planned to include in the play (e.g.: "Henry and Bertha—the nag, at home in suburbia. They argue. Henry can't take it anymore. He leaves.") I also typed the one scene that had been dictated so far, so I could pass it out to the kids and talk about the problems we were encountering. Jason was back, and was not at all pleased with the job Randy had done on Henry Sneed ("he's just not like that"). Even Randy seemed to agree. I told the kids about my own problems with what we were doing: that I felt it was impossible to keep up with them, and that I kept missing a lot of the good things they were saying. Then I asked if they would like to try a new way of working, each one writing his own scene. They were willing, so I read the cards to them, and passed them out. Here, one of those minor miracles occurred which I still can't get over: nobody wanted to work on the same scene! And Jason set to work immediately revising the scene that had been dictated.

Another problem with dictation, it doesn't give the kids a chance to write using the dramatic form. Most of the kids started writing stories. I sat down with each of them and wrote a few lines which were totally unrelated to the play. I hadn't thought about the problem before, and cursed myself for not realizing that this might be a major obstacle. But the kids are quick to point out that there's really nothing to it, and in two minutes are writing with great confidence.

I am delighted and amazed by the results. I had worried about the question of unity. But I learned that the kids were incredibly aware of, and sensitive to, each other's work. I think there are examples throughout the play of the kids picking up on each other's ideas. My favorite: in the opening line of the play, Bertha screams at Henry "I thought I told you to take out the garbage at 11:00, 1:00 and 6:00." In Howard Taikoff's scene (V), no sooner does Henry enter the house of the sexy slob maiden than he says "It's 6:00, I have to take out the garbage." Wonderful!

THE CURIOUS ADVENTURES
OF HENRY SNEED

A Play By: Jason Brill   (Scenes I & VI)
               Randy Besman   (Scene II)
               Peter Ortiz   (Scene III)
               Marianne Ettisch   (Scene IV)
               Howard Taikoff   (Scene V)

SCENE I
HENRY AND BERTHA SNEED AT THEIR HOME IN SUBURBIA.

Bertha: HENRY!! I thought I told you to take out the garbage at

	11:00, 1:00, and 6:00. Now do it, or I'm going home to mother.
Henry:	(After she screams "HENRY" he throws the newspaper in fright.) Hold it. I'm the man of this house, and I'm not going to let you push me around. Go home to mother if you want. You just married me because . . . because . . . I don't even know why.
Bertha:	Well, I never! I'm going now! Where's my suitcase?
Henry:	I got a better idea. I'll leave instead. (He packs his clothes and fishing tackle.)
Bertha:	You don't mean it, do you?
Henry:	(Henry opens the door.) But of course I mean it. If ever I come back, you had better be changed. Goodbye!! (Henry closes the door and leaves.)
Bertha:	(In distance) Henry! Henry! Come back here this instant!

SCENE II
HENRY SNEED AND HIS DOG, BUTCH, IN THE WOODS.
HENRY CARRIES A FISHING ROD AND A GUN.

Henry:	Come here, Butch.
Butch:	Arf.
Henry:	Here's a nice place to fish.
	(THREE HOURS LATER.)
Henry:	I've been sitting here for three hours and I haven't caught a thing. Hey, Butch, let's go hunting or something.
Butch:	Arf.
	HENRY AND BUTCH START HUNTING.
Henry:	(Suddenly Henry trips over a wire.) Well, somebody must have had a fence and left the wire here.
Butch:	Arf.
Henry:	This looks like a nice area to hunt. (He trips over another wire.) Hey! This wire leads to a cave. It looks like there's a road in the cave. Should we go in?
Butch:	Arf, arf.
	(THEY GO IN.)
Henry:	Hey! Look at all these lights and that board with numbers on it. What is this place? It looks like an underground space sta-

tion or something. I think we should get out!

ONE OF THE WALLS BEGINS OPENING UP.

Henry: Oh, no—the wall is opening up! It's all black, exept for one little light.

Butch: (Barking at the wall) Arf, arf, arf, arf, arf, arf. Arf.

Henry: The light's coming toward us. Wait! It looks like a big space ship or something. Wait a second, now the door is opening up!

OUT POPS AN INSTRUCTION BOOK. HENRY CATCHES IT IN HIS HANDS.

Henry: (Reading)   If you want to get away
                          from something or other,
                 Get in this ship
                          but not with another.

Do I really want to go away? Leave my wife and everything. I guess I could go away and come right back. I'd have to leave Butch.

Butch: (Sadly) Arf, arf. . . .

Henry: I guess I'll go for maybe just a day. (Henry gets in spaceship.) Goodbye, Butch, I won't be gone long. You know the way home. Goodbye, Butch, goodbye.

THE DOOR OF THE SPACESHIP CLOSES.

Computer: Hello.

Henry: (Turning around very quickly) Who's there?

Computer: I am your computer, Stewardess, and co-pilot.

Henry: Could you tell me where we are going?

Computer: Well did you press the N or the S button?

Henry: I pressed the N button.

Computer: Good then you're going to the south which is Neatling land.

Henry: What would happen if I had pressed the S button?

Computer: You would have gone to a place called the land of the Slobs, where everybody does nothing but lie around eating all day.

Henry: Boy, I'm glad I didn't go there. How long will this trip to the land of the Neatlings take?

Computer: About 10 more seconds. 10, 9, 8, 7, 6, 5, 4, 3, 2, 1.

HENRY LEAVES THE SHIP AND GOES TO NEATLING LAND

HENRY SNEED IN THE CASTLE OF THE KING OF THE LAND OF SLOBS AND THE NEATLINGS.

(Henry walks into the King's Castle. The Slobs and the Neatlings take him to the King.)

King:	Who are you?
Henry:	I'm Henry Sneed.
Slobs and Neatlings:	King, let's torture him.
King:	Wait. What do you want?
Henry:	I was fishing and I got lost.
King:	Take him to a room.
Henry:	No, wait! I want to go home! I want to go home!
King:	First, tell me about America.
Henry:	It's divided into little towns. All kinds of people live there. Except for Neatlings and Slobs. Some are good. They're kind.
King:	Nice land. Lots of food. Right?
Henry:	Yep! But wait. I want you to tell me about your land.
King:	Part of it is clean. Some of it is dirty.
Henry:	Got any water?
King:	Dirty or clean?
Henry:	Clean! Hey, are there any girls?
King:	Yes. Some are pretty. Some are not.
Henry:	Does it rain here?
King:	Cats and dogs. The cats are Neatlings; they keep where they sleep clean. The dogs are Slobs; they leave all the dirt around.
Henry:	Got any tough dogs?
King:	Just one, the guard. His name's Petorama.
Henry:	What a weird name. My dog's named Butch.
King:	That's even a weirder name.
Henry:	How do people live?
King:	The men and the women live separately. There's only one kid, mine. My name's Pejaranhow, and my kid's name is Pejaranhow, Jr. He'll be the joker when he grows up. My daughter will be the king when I die. Her name is Marivickianne.
Henry:	Why do the men and women live separately?

King:	They live separately because the boys are too fresh. Everyone else will die except for my family. Pejaranhow, Jr. and Marivickianne will get married. He'll be the queen and she'll be the king and then their son will be the joker. Their name when they are married will be Marivickiannepejaranhow.
Henry:	What a weird name. My son's name is only Tom.
King:	Hey, that's a weird name.
Henry:	Got any stores?
King:	Yes.
Henry:	What do they sell?
King:	Bats, rats, cockroaches.
Henry:	Whoops! I'm not hungry.
King:	And I was going to ask you to dinner!
Henry:	No. I'm not hungry.
Neatlings and Slobs:	Can we torture him now?
King:	No. First he must eat, because I'm the King.
Henry:	I think I better be going.
King:	Eat! Eat!
Henry:	I don't have to eat.
King:	I am the King, so eat.
Henry:	Bye now!
King:	Get him! Get him!

(HENRY RUNS)

Neatlings and Slobs: We lost him. We lost him.

SCENE IV
HENRY SNEED AND A BEAUTIFUL NEATLING MAIDEN

(When Henry meets the Neatling Maiden, he is walking down a Neatling road and he gets stunned by seeing her.)

Henry:	(He says to her) You're the most stunning creature I've seen yet. What's your name?
Neatling Maiden:	Why, my name is Carnation Neatling, and I live in the mushroom Neatling house over there. Would you like to come in and have some Neatling tea?

(While they are having tea, Henry says:)

Henry:	I can't get over how beautiful you are. Are all Neatling women like you?
Carnation:	Not all. Only the Neatling virgins.
Henry:	What do you mean? Are you a. . ., a. . ., a. . .?
Carnation:	Yes, Henry, I am.
Henry:	By the way, do you have a family? Do you live with anyone?
Carnation:	No. I have no one except my Neatling dog, rabbit, guinea pigs. Their hair is white like a daisy.
Henry:	How come they call you Carnation? —even though you look like one a little.
Carnation:	I can't talk to you anymore. I think you better go. (As she locks the door on his face, he's outside—)
Henry:	Wait, Carnation. I want to ask you something. . .
	But, as he says that, THE MUSHROOM HOUSE DISAPPEARS.
Carnation:	(Out of a Blue Moon) Oh, Henry, how loving you are. Oh my darling. I am a bla bla bla so I can't have you near. Even though my heart desires so. How can I tell you my feelings.
Henry:	Oh, please, Carnation, come out from hiding. You're as pretty as a carnation.

NEXT DAY

Carnation:	(She was cleaning her mushroom house when someone touches her and she jumps.) OH! You scared me. I told you not to come.
Henry:	But Carnation, I love you. Will you marry me? I don't know what I'd do without you and your beauty.
Carnation:	But Henry. . . I like you, but. . . you're much much too dirty, and you. . . Oh, good bye.

SCENE V
HENRY SNEED AND A SEXY SLOB MAIDEN.

Henry:	(Walking and looking all around. Suddenly he falls, he tripped over a hunk of dust. It wasn't dust. It was a Slob Maiden.) Hellow there.
Slob Maiden:	H$_e$llllloo$_o$oo. My house is over there.
Henry:	Excuse me?
Slob Maiden:	(Whispers, aside) He's not my type, but he'll do. I'll just fix him up a little.

Henry:	Are you married?
Slob Maiden:	No, but I was divorced five times. I'm getting married.
Henry:	Congratulations. Who are you going to marry?
Slob Maiden:	(Whispers) Oh, boy!
	(THEY WENT TO THE HOUSE.)
Henry:	Cough, cough. I see you're allowed to smoke.
Slob Maiden:	(Whispers) HELP!
Henry:	(Enters the house) It's 6:00, I have to take out the garbage.
Slob Maiden:	No! No! Don't you like the smell of banana peels and tin cans, bone, vegetable, dead cats, milk.
	(Aside) Oh boy! Is he goofed up!
Slob Maiden:	(Whispers, for the second time) Oh boy! Is he goofed up!
Henry:	Can I have the Newspaper?
Slob Maiden:	Yeh. It's on the front lawn.
Henry:	(Goes to the front lawn, but there wasn't any.) (Aside, he whispers:) Now where is the front lawn? All I see is brown and black weeds. That must be the lawn, but is she ever sloppy.
	(While Henry was talking to himself about the slob maiden, she was talking about Henry. All the other boy husbands ran away as soon as they looked or went in the house.)
Henry:	What happened to your other husbands?
Slob Maiden:	Oh, I'll tell you. The first one was named Petep. He smelled the house and he ran away! Then Jackettwa ran away from me! Then Dragold ran from the mice! Then, last, but not least, Rickerity ran from the lawn!
Henry:	What a lawn!
Slob Maiden:	How dare you insult me!
Henry:	Who, me? I'm not holding it in any more. You are a slob!
Slob Maiden:	Why do you think I'm called a Slob Maiden, clean boy?
Henry:	I hate you. Good bye!
Slob Maiden:	Good bye!

SCENE VI
HENRY AND BERTHA SNEED BACK HOME IN SUBURBIA

(There is a knock on the door.)

Bertha:	Who is it? (She opens the door. Sees Henry. Screams with joy and starts crying.) Henry, you're home. Oh, how much I've missed you.
Henry:	It's good to see you too. I guess I did love you, but didn't know it.
Bertha:	I'll never nag you again. Oh, Henry!
Henry:	I was hoping you'd say that.
Bertha:	Where have you been for three years?
Henry:	You'd never believe me.
Bertha:	Yes, I will.
Henry:	Oh, OK. I've been with Slobs and Neatlings.
Bertha:	What are they?
Henry:	Well, there are two different kinds of people, and very weird, especially the girls. OOPS!
Bertha:	What girls? (With a mean eye)
Henry:	Slob and Neatling Maidens.
Bertha:	Well, I guess so. I mean, what else can you do for three years?
Henry:	I was thinking of never coming back, but I got so fed up with the extremes. So I came back. Let's never fight again.
	(AND SO THEY LIVED HAPPILY EVER AFTER. OR SO WE THINK.)
Bertha:	Henry!! I thought I told you to take out the garbage at 11:00, 1:00, and . . .

THE END

Discovering our World Neighbors

I asked the kids whether they would like to work together again on another large project, like the play, or whether they would like to go back to working on their own. With the exception of Ann, who was anxious to get back to her story, everyone wanted to do more writing together. So I said I had one idea that we might try: to write our own geography book—a crazy geography, of course, in keeping with the present mood of the school. I believe the kids were really quite excited by the idea, and we even talked about giving the book to Miss Kintisch as a present, since, at various times during the year, she has expressed some concern about these kids not keeping up with their regular geography lessons. The Geography book could be our way of showing we had not forgotten the subject completely, and we decided to begin next week.

To prepare for the project I stopped by Miss Kintisch's room to ask if I could borrow a geography text for a few days. To the great credit of the social studies department at I.S. 70, the standard texts are no longer being used in classrooms. There were many in storage, however, and Miss Kintisch gave me the key to a closet filled with history, social studies and geography texts. I had trouble figuring out which, if any, of the books were actually written for sixth graders, but then I decided it really didn't matter anyway. I took four or five books from the shelves and headed home for a night of pleasant reading.

Reading the books, I discovered they really haven't changed. I looked over two or three of the most recently revised texts (1965, I believe). There was Africa, still the dark, sleepy continent, or is it giant? And, in one book, the section on Africa had a frontpiece picturing an English princess, on an official visit according to the caption, seated on a throne with the tribal chiefs at her feet. And these books must still be in use in schools all over the city!

Best to stay away from those controversial countries anyway—China, Russia, Africa—where the textbook writers fill page after page by conscientiously skirting all the most pertinent issues. Best to find some neutral country about which they have next to nothing to say. Ah, Australia!

"Australia is South of the equator."

"When it is summer in the United States, it is winter in Australia."

"Most of Australia suffers from insufficient rainfall."

"In the grassland areas, Australian ranches suffer from the problem of draught."

I went through the various chapters on Australia quite carefully, took down the major paragraph headings, such as "The Land," "The People," "Industry," "Agricultrue,"—and a few sample sentences from each paragraph. I typed these on separate 3 x 5 cards, just as I had done with the separate scenes in the play, so the kids could have a choice of topics when we passed the cards around.

I also started thinking about nonsense words, for they can come in handy when constructing a country. Then I remembered that once, during a freshman composition course, in response to an absolutely horrendous assignment (we were supposed to write a factual description of a scientific experiment) I discovered in the back of my old Webster's Collegiate (published in 1932) a Glossary of Scottish Words and Phrases. Fantastic words! I scattered them throughout my essay: "I placed the warm, goustrous solution of spurtle on the windowsill overnight to munt."—etc. So I decided to make a special geographical dictionary for the kids using some of these words. No definitions, of course, just an alphabetical listing: blitter, brak, bummle, braxy, begunk, etc.

We began work on the geography book in earnest, sort of. Distributing the paragraph headings was no problem—the kids really do have definite preferences when it comes to choosing a topic to write about, and there were more than enough topics to go around. But the dictionary proved to be such an overwhelming success that we never really started writing. Instead, the kids sat down with each other and started to read and laugh over the words. Then, completely on their own, they started to add their own nonsense words. I was nonplussed, never having expected such a response. And, frankly, a little worried about the geography book, which seemed to have been completely forgotten. But I couldn't deny that the class was great fun, and I guess somewhere in the back of my mind I decided that sooner or later the kids would get over their fascination with the dictionary and begin writing. (Throughout the three or four weeks that we worked on the geography book, by the way, I was never able to make enough copies of the dictionary for the kids. They wrote and doodled on them, added words, underlined words that they were particularly fond of, and carried them off to their friends. It was the single most popular thing I ever printed for the kids.)

During the next session, the kids came up with a name for their country—"Withershins," and they did begin writing. The tendency, however, was to make every other word a nonsense word—the dictionary was still the primary focus. I thought it might be useful to demonstrate a more modest technique for using nonsense, that is, how it is possible to take a single word and attach a variety of meanings to it, while never actually defining the word. So I wrote a short paragraph about "dunsh," which comes from dunsh piles, naturally, is gathered by the old women of Withershins, and refined in factories which pollute half the countryside. Then I got carried away and started writing suggested activities "for extra credit"—that section that appears in the back of almost every chapter in every textbook I've ever seen:

> Take a field trip to the nearest swamp. Look for piles of dunsh. Did you find any? No, of course you didn't! It grows only in Withershins. Write a long report about your discoveries.

Eventually, I read what I had written to the kids. Then I asked "What is dunsh?" No one knew. So I asked, "where is it found?"—in swamps, in Withershins. "Who gathers it?"—the old women. "Where do they take it?" —to factories, etc. etc. So we discovered that we knew a lot about dunsh without actually knowing what it was.

An amazing session, I don't think I said a word to the kids who were working on the geography book. They came in, picked up extra copies of the dictionary, and began talking and writing by themselves. So I spent the session talking mostly to Ann about her story, her plans for the summer, next year, etc. At the end of the period, the kids handed me about four or five pages. I was particularly pleased with Dina Venezia's writing. She had picked her nonsense words so carefully, giving so much attention to their sound. For example, she wrote about a lake in Withershins called the Curmurring Caber— such a beautiful name for a lake. Her mountains are called the Gawsey Geks. And throughout her work there is a subtle, deadpan humour that I find quite exceptional: "Crouchies are ugly little things that are delicious when you cover them with bread crumbs and boil them in cold water."

We had one more writing session, then I mimeographed copies of the book for the kids and passed them out. We gave copies to Miss Kintisch, who laughed and was very pleased.

The kids told me they thought it was the best writing that they had ever done. And, while I don't think I agree with their assessment, it certainly was a joyful way to end the year.

DISCOVERING OUR WORLD NEIGHBORS

A SIXTH GRADE GEOGRAPHY BOOK

by: Marianne Ettisch Victoria Larkin
 Peter Ortiz Howard Taikoff
 Jason Brill Dina Venezia

THE LAND OF WITHERSHINS

The Great Fissenless Frample

In the western half of Withershins there is a desert called The Great Fissenless Frample. The climate in the following parts of The Great Fissenless Frample:

North - 350° F.
South - 375° below 0
East -- 40° F.
West - 875° F.

Sometimes it rains in the Great Fissenless Frample. Sometimes it rains with special chemicals. One day a week it rains to help the crouchies grow, then another day to help the quaichies grow.

Crouchies are ugly little things which are delicious when you cover them with breadcrumbs and boil them in cold water. They can't grow unless it rains a certain chemical. The chemical, as it approaches the crouchies, it makes them sprout out seeds. The seeds then dig into the ground and grow within one day.

When it rains a certain chemical the quaichies all pop out of the ground and land in the main plant. The plant then grows. The quaichies are delicious when you boil them in hot water and then roll them in mud.

Lakes

There is a lake in Withershins called Curmurring Caber. The temperature is approximately 850°F. The water is yellow, orange, and red and always looks like it's on fire. In the water live Ettles which are red, yellow, and orange. They feed on little plants on the bottom of the 350 foot lake.

Mountains

The Gawsey Geks are the biggest mountains in Withershins. They range in sizes from 2 feet to 4 feet. At the top they are 450° below 0 and at the bottom they are 449° F. The Gawsey Geks are in the middle of Withershins and surround the Curmurring Caber.

The Great Fissenless Frample,
Lakes, and Mountains
by Dina Venezia

Map of Withershins with The Great Fissenless Frample

by Marianne Ettisch

HISTORY OF TOWNS IN WITHERSHINS

(Towns are listed in order of foundation.)

Stibblerig (Pronounced Stibbelrig) was founded (in our time) in 1603. It has a population of 200 people (men, women, and children). In the main part of the town there are three main gruttens. The other gruttens (not included in the three main gruttens) are for odds and ends like argles and fards and carshes. There are only two clud stations, two movie theatres, one stage theatre, three baghash gruttens, one sitnal grutten, one big aff grutten, one herry, and three clekits, plus one very large, fresh gurr and grutten. There are only 29 mushtrolls in Stibblerig.
Pillpov was founded (again in our time) in 1622. It has a population of 357

people (the population count always includes all men, women and children). Pillpov is one of the only towns in Withershins where you can buy gurgles, and everyone *loves* gurgles! Everyone in Pillpov usually travels to Stibblerig for the ODDS and ENDS so therefore Pillpov has only 4 gruttens. There are only 32 mushtrolls in Pillpov.

Lichwakē was founded (in our time) in 1629 and it has a population of 220 people. There are only 70 mushtrolls there. Lichwakē is famous for its pawk loshes where you can buy pluffs, mims, and mizzles. A pluff is like a little white fuzzy ball of rickle and it has 2 small ickers.

History of towns by Victoria Larkin

INDUSTRY IN WITHERSHINS

There are clug factories that make lots of clug and when they burn it, it turns to clugier. The main branch that makes clug is Clugfuffle. The manager is Cugclear Clufman. You find clug in the ground. You drill for it. The clug factories make low lead clug. They sell it at Clesso.

by Howard Taikoff

RELIGION IN WITHERSHINS

The religion in Withershins is Betrusminy. This is a prejudice.

by Randy Besman

MINING IN WITHERSHINS

The major mining fields are for (and especially) rivers which are red with 3½ legs sticking out of its awnie which makes it look something like a dindle. Another major thing that we mine for in Withershins is a wemmelwarsal. This is a gold colored thing that looks somewhat like a Terge with antennae. Of the newer mines there are antenumps. They are very valuable because if you don't have antenump you can't live in Withershins. Antemumps are holes with walls around them, they are usually furnished with dooks and fendys. You sleep in dooks with assorted fendys around the house for sitting.

One of the biggest jobs for Withershinians is mining for antenumps. It also pays well in flinks.

by Jason Brill

THE GOVERNMENT OF WITHERSHINS

Withershins has 24 Kings and they are very good enemies. The people are always voting for the bad king. The king lives in the royal dungeon. The capitol is Zillabony. Every year they kill the king then they give the dog the bones.

by Peter Ortiz

HOW WELL DID YOU READ?

Question: Who made the first Grushie?
Answer: Withershins Garguffle.

Question: Who discovered Smedderdumm?
Answer: Vivers Wooerbab.

Question: What is the history of Withershins?
Answer: In the beginning there were slicklestompernickerstolings and then the present . . .

Question: Who griblinked the first octupucle?
Answer: Lillier Trasidone in 30.D.

ON YOUR OWN

1. Get 27 Braxy's and Balloot them. For extra credit write a report on how the Withershinians manufacture them.

2. Go buy some dunsh and give it to your friends. Tell them that it tastes better in Withershins and then sell the rest and go to Withershins.

Bibliography

The Pennsylvania State University and Duke University libraries both house large collections of Utopian literature. Each publishes a check list of its collection and I would refer any teacher who is interested in obtaining a comprehensive bibliography to these two sources:

Listing of Utopias and Fantastic Voyages
Rare Books and Special Collections
W342 Pattee Library
The Pennsylvania State Unviersity
University Park, Pennsylvania

Professor Glenn Negley
Duke University
Durham, North Carolina

If you stretch the definition of Utopias as I did, it is necessary to add innumerable children's stories, fairy tales and myths, a whole body of science fiction works, and the many published accounts of life in real utopian communities. This would mean an immense and rather useless bibliography, and besides I'm not about to embark on such a project. The brief list of titles which follows, then, is made up quite simply of some of my favorite works, or of works which I found particularly useful in my teaching.

Negley, Glenn and J. Max Patrick. *The Quest for Utopia: An Anthology of Imaginary Societies.* (Paperback.) A fine, scholarly introduction to Utopian literature, containing many selections, interesting biographical and historical commentaries, and an excellent bibliography of Utopian works published since 1850. This work may be more interesting as a general reference work for teachers than for use directly in the classroom.

Burgess, Anthony. *A Clockwork Orange* (Paperback.) Language is a problem. Burgess imagines a grim future for England, dominated by street gangs whose language is heavily spiced with Russian idioms. A glossary of terms is included but in my opinion the whole idea is rather exasperating, and obscures the most interesting things about the work.

Butler, Samuel. *Erewhon.* (Paperback.)

deBergerac, Cyrano (Savinien). *The Comical History of the States and Empire of the Worlds of the Moon and Suns.* Translated by Richard Aldington.

Carroll, Lewis. *Alice in Wonderland, Through the Looking Glass, Sylvie and Bruno.* Inspired nonsense, as everyone knows.

Goodman, Paul. *Utopian Essays and Practical Proposals, Communitas.*

Huxley, Aldous. *Ape and Essence, Brave New World, Island,* (Paperback.) (See diaries on RELIGION.) Of these works, *Brave New World* may be the most useful in the classroom. Particularly for initiating discussion and/or writing on entertainment, sexual mores, childbirth, and, of course, drugs.

Kafka, Franz. *Amerika.* (Paperback.) Hardly a Utopia, but, after all, Kafka had never seen America and the descriptions of New York City, the surrounding countryside, a political campaign, and other details of American life are truly fascinating.

Lewis, C.S. *The Chronicles of Narnia.* (Six books, paperbakc.) See TRAVELling to an imaginary land.

London, Jack. *The Iron Heel.* A poorly written, horribly sentimental, but interesting work, it portrays an aboritve street revolution (in Chicago!) and the growth of an American oligarchy. Definitely not the Jack London I learned about in school. Might be interesting for a group of politically active kids.

Michaux, Henri. *Collected Works.* Translated by Richard Ellman. (Paperback.) A number of imaginary worlds are included here ("In the Land of the Hacs," "The Hivinizikis") which are at once humorous and disturbing. Mi-

109

chaux's worlds are written as prose poems, short, pithy, easily accessible to kids. Five stars.

Neill, A.S. *The Last Man Alive.* (Paperback.) A whimsical story featuring Neill himself and his students as characters. Neill made up this story with a group of his students at Summerhill. The children's delightful comments concerning Neill's ability as a storyteller are included in the text.

Orwell, George. *1984.* (Paperback.)

Plato. *The Republic.* (Paperback.) Difficult for younger readers, but the discussion of various forms of government (oligarchy, timarchy, democracy, tyranny) may be of interest. Also valuable may be Plato's ideas concerning state control of the arts. I've always been particularly interested in those sections in which Plato proposes censoring huge portions of the epic poems of Homer.

Swift, Jonathan. *Gulliver's Travels.* (Paperback.) The "Voyage to the Country of the Houyhnhnms" must contain the best "reverse" view of western civilization as seen from an imaginary place in the whole of Utopian literature. It is difficult to know how to introduce children to the work of Swift, however, since the language is difficult and sophisticated. Text book anthologists have taken advantage of this for years, simplifying the language while heavily censoring the work. At one point I had hoped to tape readings from *Gulliver's Travels* for children to listen to.

Vonnegut, Kurt, Jr. *Cat's Cradle, Slaughterhouse Five,* and others. (Paperback.) See WAR.

Welles, H.G. *The Time Machine.* (Paperback.) See TRAVELLING TO AN IMAGINARY LAND.

At the beginning of the Utopias project I spent a good deal of time reviewing many of the histories of real Utopian settlements, such as Charles Nordoff's *Communistic Societies in the United States,* and Everett Weber's *Escape to Utopia.* The books were interesting to me, but on the whole rather dry and scholarly, and I was never able to find any way to relate my reading of them to my work in the classroom. I found works of fiction far more appropriate. This is not to say, however, that another teacher in another situation wouldn't find works of this kind perfectly useful.

Please remember that this is a library book,
and that it belongs only temporarily to each
person who uses it. Be considerate. Do
not write in this, or any, library book.

DATE DUE